An Archaeology of Nat

In studying settlements and monuments, archaeologists have learnt a great deal about the ways in which these sites were used during prehistory. But such studies have often been limited, for their main sources of evidence were purposefully created. Little has been said about the special importance to prehistoric people of *unaltered* features of the landscape.

This volume explores why natural places such as caves, mountains, springs and rivers assumed a sacred character in European prehistory, and how the evidence for this can be analysed in the field. It shows how established research on votive deposits, rock art and production sites can contribute to a more imaginative approach to the prehistoric landscape, and can even shed light on the origins of monumental architecture. The discussion is illustrated through a wide range of European examples, and three extended case studies.

An Archaeology of Natural Places extends the range of landscape studies and makes the results of modern research accessible to a wider audience, including students and academics, field archaeologists, and those working in heritage management.

Richard Bradley is Professor of Archaeology at Reading University. His main interests are prehistoric social and landscape archaeology and rock art. Among his recent books are *The Significance of Monuments, Rock Art and the Prehistory of Atlantic Europe* and *Altering the Earth*.

An Archaeology of Natural Places

Richard Bradley

 Routledge
Taylor & Francis Group

LONDON AND NEW YORK

First published 2000
by Routledge
2 Park Square, Milton Park, Abingdon, Oxon OX14 4RN

Simultaneously published in the USA and Canada
by Routledge
270 Madison Avenue, New York, NY 10016

Reprinted 2002, 2004, 2006

Transferred to Digital Printing 2007

Routledge is an imprint of the Taylor & Francis Group, an informa business

Typeset in Baskerville by RefineCatch Limited, Bungay, Suffolk

Printed and bound by CPI Group (UK) Ltd, Croydon, CR0 4YY

British Library Cataloguing in Publication Data
A catalogue record for this book is available from the British Library

Library of Congress Cataloguing in Publication Data
Bradley, Richard, 1946–
　　An archaeology of natural places / Richard Bradley.
　　　　p.　　cm.
　　Includes bibliographical references and index.
　　ISBN 0–415–22149–8 – ISBN 0–415–22150–1 (pbk)
　　1. Prehistoric peoples – Europe.　2. Sacred space – Europe.
　　3. Landscape assessment – Europe.
　　4. Europe – Antiquities.　I. Title.
GN803.B658　2000
936 – dc21　　　　　　　　　　　　　　　　99–042197

ISBN10: 0–415–22149–8 (hbk)
ISBN10: 0–415–22150–1 (pbk)

ISBN13: 978–0–415–22149–8 (hbk)
ISBN13: 978–0–415–22150–4 (pbk)

Publisher's Note
The publisher has gone to great lengths to ensure the quality
of this reprint but points out that some imperfections in
the original may be apparent

For my friends in Scandinavia

A Saami *siejdde* associated with sacrifices of fish
at Alta, Finmark, northern Norway

Contents

Illustrations

Figures

Tables

Preface

In one sense this book caught me by surprise. It reflects on the results of research carried out over more than fifteen years, but locates them in a framework of which I have only recently become fully aware. In another sense, it is the result of a quite specific stimulus: a visit to the north of Norway to attend the Alta Conference on Rock Art in 1993. After the formal proceedings were over, a number of us travelled around Finmark under the guidance of Reidun Andreassen and Audhild Schanche, and had the opportunity to see and discuss some of the sacred places of the Saami. They came as a revelation to someone brought up on the monuments of western Europe, for very few of these were marked in a conventional way. They made me more aware of the unaltered places that are so often missing from the landscape archaeology of other parts of Europe. They also suggested a new perspective on my own studies of rock carvings, votive deposits and axe production sites. It is an approach that has come to dominate my current field-work in Spain, conducted jointly with Rámon Fábregas and Germán Delibes. I have also had the good fortune to visit rock art sites in Spain and Portugal with Javier Costas, Felipe Criado, Maria de Jesus Sanches and Paula Mota Santos, and this experience has influenced my thinking too.

The opportunity to develop these impressions came during a period of research leave from Reading University in autumn 1998, when I was able to visit the universities of Bergen, Lund and Tromsø. During these visits I had the chance to talk to many people about their work, to visit a number of major sites and to consult sources that were not available in Britain. Among the many people who helped me with this project were Knut Andreas Bergsvik, Jan Magne Gjerde, Cecilie Larsen, Trond Lødøen and Gro Mandt in Bergen, Lars Larsson and the graduate students in Lund and, in Tromsø, Knut Helsgog, Anders Hesjedal, Bjornar Olsen, Poul Simonsen, Stine Benedicte Steen and Inger Storli. I also learned much of interest from an earlier visit to Gothenburg organised by Kristian Kristiansen and Jarl Nordbladh, and from conversations with Neil Price in Uppsala and Flemming Kaul in Copenhagen. It is only right that the book should be dedicated to 'my friends in Scandinavia'.

Back in Britain, parts or all of the text have been read by Lara Alves, Martin Henig, Andy Jones and Sturt Manning, and I am grateful to them all for their

comments and good advice. I must also thank Knut Andreas Bergsvik, Trond
Lødøen, the Ashmolean Museum, Oxford, and the Pitt Rivers Museum, Oxford,
for providing plates and for allowing me to reproduce them here. An earlier
version of part of Chapter 9 was published in the *Oxford Journal of Archaeology*, and
I am grateful to the editors and publisher for permission to use this material in the
book. All the original artwork is by Mel Costello. He has been helpful, creative
and wonderfully efficient. The quality of his drawings speaks for itself, and the
appearance of my originals must remain a secret.

This is a book that could have been much longer and might have extended
beyond the limits of prehistoric Europe. In principle, it could have been written
about any part of the world – or, indeed, about the world as a whole. But it
seemed important to keep the text as brief and accessible as possible, while providing pointers to other approaches through an extensive bibliography. In this respect
it is really a companion volume to *The Significance of Monuments* published by
Routledge in 1998, and I have tried to emphasise that connection by employing a
similar format. This was not my objective from the outset, and in this, as in so
much else, the growth of this book has taken me entirely by surprise.

Surely that is the pleasure of doing archaeology?

Part I

Introductions

Limestone uplands like the Pennines plus a small region of igneous rocks with at least one extinct volcano. A precipitous and indented sea-coast.

W.H. Auden's conception of Eden, from *The Dyer's Hand and Other Essays* (1968), quoted by permission of Faber and Faber

In the cave of thunder

Sacred places in a northern landscape

The book begins with Sir Arthur Evans, one of the most famous archaeologists of the twentieth century. As a young man he excavated a Saami sacrificial site in Finland. This chapter discusses the ethnography of northern hunters and reindeer herders, and reviews what is known about such places today. It discusses their role in Saami perceptions of the world, and considers their implications for studies of the ancient landscape. In doing so, Chapter I introduces the idea of an archaeology of 'natural places'. It concludes by describing the structure of the book and summarising the contents of the different sections.

A traveller's tale

In a lake in the north of Finland there is an island 'shaped like a giant tortoise' (Figure 1). It contains a sacrificial cave venerated by the local people. In 1873, during a storm that threatened his boat, an Oxford undergraduate made his way to the site. Perhaps it is not surprising that the island was sacred to the thunder god (Itkonen 1944: 3–4).

On the steep flank of that island, Ukonsaari, was a shallow cave, although in fact it was little more than a small cleft in the rock face. It had supposedly been 'used by the Lapps [Saami] as an offering-place'. Certainly, it was filled with bones. The roof of the cave was coated in soot, suggesting that it was still in use, and some of the burnt food that the visitor found was obviously of recent origin.

In a way that would be unthinkable today, he immediately decided to dig. Beneath the floor of the cave the bones were older, and he could identify the remains of reindeer and bear as well as other species. That was interesting in itself, but as he was preparing to leave, he came upon a deposit of charcoal, and in this he identified a metal ornament that he believed might date from the Bronze Age. Like the bones, it had apparently been burnt. Below this deposit there were human remains. He took the ornament, an 'ear-ring', home with him, together with a sample of the other relics.

We know what he found on Ukonsaari because he described the cave in a letter to his step-mother, who copied his account into a notebook which still survives. She was used to discoveries of this kind, for she was married to Sir John Evans,

Figure 1   Arthur Evans's sketch of Ukonsaari, Finland
Source: Reproduced by permission of the Pitt Rivers Museum, Oxford

one of the founders of British archaeology. He was the first person to systematise what was known about prehistoric artefacts in this country and a collector of antiquities in his own right. His son had obviously inherited his interest in the past (Brown 1993: 11–19; Evans 1943: 174).

That visitor to the island was Arthur Evans, who was later to become one of the best-known archaeologists of his day, although the work for which he is most famous was to take place in the Mediterranean. In his early twenties, he was already adept at handling archaeological evidence. He noted that the cave on Ukonsaari was too small to have been inhabited, and in any case it was open to the elements. Its contents had an unusual character too, for there were no long bones among the animal remains, and fish bones were apparently absent even though fishing played a prominent role in the local economy. Still more striking, there were no antlers in the cave, although they had been deposited in large numbers on the rocks outside it. That was particularly significant, as he discovered that the local inhabitants used to arrange these antlers in a circle in honour of Ukon, the god of thunder, winds and lakes.

His interpretation was clear: no one could have lived in the cave because of its unusual topography. Its contents may not have been the remains of ordinary meals because of the ways in which the bones had been selected, and the 'ear-ring' was unlikely to have been lost by chance, especially as it seemed to have been placed in a fire. The collection of antlers found outside the cave recalled the offerings associated with Ukon. For Evans it was confirmation that this was a sacrificial site. How would we understand it today?

Saami sacred geography

There are two ways of introducing the archaeology of natural places. One is by extending the chronological and geographical framework of this chapter to take in other cases. The alternative (which I prefer) is to consider how much is really known about the phenomenon that Evans encountered on the island of Ukonsaari. I shall consider an example from his later career in Chapter 2.

The cave that Evans investigated in Finland can now be recognised as one of a series of sacrificial sites made by the native inhabitants of northern Scandinavia. Although some of the metal items found at these sites originated in distant parts of Europe (the silver ear-ring was from Russia), the main feature of these places was an extensive deposit of animal bones. The meat bones were inside the cave, whilst the antlers were found outside it. Saami metal deposits are not Bronze Age, as Evans believed, but date from a relatively short period between AD 1000 and 1350 (Zachrisson 1984). As his experience shows, the sites themselves were obviously used over a longer period.

In fact there seems little doubt that the Saami and neighbouring groups of hunters and reindeer herders were the indigenous inhabitants of northern Scandinavia. Prehistoric rock carvings show what seem to be the shamans' drums for which the Saami were famous before the arrival of Christian missionaries. These carvings also illustrate the special importance of the bear, which is a notable feature of Saami ethnography (Helsgog 1987). In the same way, the Mesolithic burials at Olenii Ostrov in Karelia recall a number of features that are recorded among northern hunter gatherers, including the siting of the cemetery on an island. The artefacts from the graves recall the importance of elks and snakes in local systems of belief, and ancient rock carvings found in the same region conform to the symbolic system of the recent inhabitants of the area. Marek Zvelebil (1997) concludes that elements of a traditional cosmology lapsed at different times in different parts of northern Europe: they lasted into the mid-first millennium AD in Karelia, they were eliminated by Christian missionaries in northern Scandinavia in the seventeenth and eighteenth centuries but they still survived until modern times in part of western Siberia.

This suggests that the deposition of metalwork on the island of Ukonsaari represented just one episode in a much longer history of ritual associated with natural places. This is certainly consistent with what is known today about sacred sites in the landscape.

The positions of more than 500 of these are now known (Manker 1957; Mulk 1994 and 1996). They are generally found at striking features of the natural terrain. Although some of these were inaccessible and could be reached only by those who knew where to find them, others were closely associated with the wider pattern of movement about the country. Some cult places served an entire community, whilst others were located along the routes by which people travelled at different times of the year. They might be visited by groups who followed the same paths or fished in the same lakes, but every family also had its sacred mountain where it provided offerings; sometimes the sacrificial site was located just below the summit (Rydving 1995). The main features to be treated in this way were (in descending order of frequency): hills and mountains, lakes, peninsulas, caves, islands, waterfalls and springs. A few offerings were also made in areas of pasture, but these places do not seem to have been distinguished by natural landmarks of the same kind. The sacrificial sites are generally known as *siejddes*. They are nearly all places that seem to be distinguished from the surrounding landscape by their striking topography. These features were not altered by the activities that took place there, and the rock formations that are such a conspicuous feature of *siejddes* were rarely modified by any form of structure, although some examples in the north of Scandinavia were enclosed by a low wall surmounted by brushwood, whilst others were ringed by a circle of antlers. In these cases, the main focus was sometimes a cairn (Manker 1957: 300–1; Vorren and Eriksen 1993).

The *siejddes* are often characterised by rock formations that bear a certain resemblance to humans, animals or birds (Figure 2). These features were retained in their original forms and the shapes of these outcrops were never changed. '[They] were not of monumental character, and thus did not express the idea that humans were in any way above nature' (Schanche in Mulk 1994: 122). Manker makes a similar point when he says that '[the Lapps] let the gods choose their own shape' (Manker 1957: 306). At the same time, it is clear that some of these stones have other obvious characteristics. They might be particularly massive or they could be an unusual colour. Some of the most distinctive were blocks that had been split open during cold weather to provide fissures or natural portals leading into the surface of the rock.

The sacrificial sites might be distinguished from the other parts of the landscape by their striking appearance, but they also included a variety of idols (Manker 1957). These were formed of two raw materials – stone and wood – both of which were very common in the natural world. Unworked stones were brought into service as idols, either because of their unusual colour or raw material or more often because their distinctive shapes resembled those of living beings. Some of these were introduced to the site, but it was extremely rare for them to be modified in any way.

There were also a number of wooden idols, although it is harder to decide how common these once were because so few have survived to the present day. The wooden idols were often carved out of the boles of trees, but even when this happened their forms were not altered materially. In fact it seems quite likely that these pieces were selected because their shapes already suggested the figures of deities.

Manker (1957) provides some interesting statistics on the character of both

Figure 2 The natural setting of a Saami siejdde at
Alta, Finmark, northern Norway

groups of idols. The commonest form was that of a human figure, and surviving images are more frequent in stone than in wood. Figures of animals are less often found. Virtually all of these were made of stone. In only two cases were naturally shaped pieces changed by carving. Like the siejddes, some of these attracted attention because of their shapes or colours. There are also cases where different materials were combined to imitate the separate parts of the body. For example, a deity could be depicted by a large, darkly coloured stone with a smaller, white stone placed on top. Some of the stone 'figures' were interpreted as the sons or servants of the thunder god or even as incarnations of the divine master of the animals.

As we have seen, the wooden idols were more complex and at least some of them had been carved. In this case there is an added complication, for living trees also seem to have been worshipped, and a number of these may have been embellished in the same way. It was common for a wooden idol to be formed from the base of the trunk. This seems to have had a special significance, as the idol was normally made by turning the raw material over, so that the roots were uppermost (Manker 1957). Such images include the thunder god who was worshipped at

Ukonsaari, and Varaldenolmmái who ensured the fertility of the reindeer and of the pastures where they fed.

The sacrifices themselves were intimately connected with the exploitation of the local landscape (Figure 3). Thus there were *siejddes* that were associated with the sacrifice of animals by hunters and herders, and others that were used for offerings of fish (Rydving 1995: 20). The animal sacrifices were generally shared with the gods. The people visiting the sacred sites consumed the meat, frequently reindeer, and left the bones, skins and antlers behind for the gods, who were capable of putting new flesh on the remains. Like the idols associated with these sites, the sacrificial rock was smeared with blood and grease, as well as fat, milk and sometimes cheese. On some sites the bones of a single reindeer were buried under a cairn beside a large boulder, but with the antlers left exposed. A similar importance attached to the killing and eating of the bear. None of its bones could be broken or discarded. Instead they were carefully collected and stored until they were eventually buried. It was a common practice in the Arctic for the bones of a sacrificed animal to be restored to their anatomical order when the remains were committed to the ground (Manker 1957).

The sacrifices were dedicated to natural forces, important in the life of the Saami, such as thunder, the winds, waters and the sun. Particular gods were associated with particular kinds of sacrifice, and to some extent the same applies to offerings that were made for different purposes. Thus black animals were sacrificed to the forces of death, and white reindeer could be offered to the sun god. Horses were sometimes sacrificed when someone was expected to die, and

Figure 3 A Saami sacrificial site as depicted by Johannes Schefferus in 1673

the thunder god might receive an uncastrated reindeer (Mulk 1996; Rydving 1995).

Decisions were reached by consulting the shamans' drums (Rydving 1995). The sound of the drum told the shaman where food could be located and allowed him to see into the past and future. Bone or brass pointers attached to the surface of the drum also provided directions. The drum offered a variety of practical information, but in some cases it instructed the Saami about the proper form of sacrifice. At times it was necessary to embark on long journeys to obtain the appropriate victims, including domesticated animals such as cattle, horses, sheep and goats, which were brought from areas a considerable distance away (Mulk 1996). The sacrificial sites were the domain of the ancestors, and all were given names. Different locations were associated with different divinities. One group of mountains might be linked with the spirits of the ancestors, whilst another might be the province of the mother goddess or of the god of thunder. Women's ancestral spirits were also associated with certain lakes.

Manker's study combined the documentary history of the Saami with an exhaustive catalogue of finds from the votive deposits themselves (Figure 4). This shows that the bones and antlers of reindeer were deposited in well over 100 different cases (Manker 1957). Domesticated animals were sacrificed at about a quarter of the sites, and bears were even less common. There was also direct evidence for the sacrifice of birds and fish.

In addition to these remains, there are numerous finds of artefacts. These include metalwork and pieces of quartz, flint and glass. Some types of metal were thought to carry special powers. Brass was sacred: it was used for the pointers on the shamans' drums and is also associated with bears' graves. Silver, which occurs more frequently in the sacrificial deposits, is never found in these burials. Many of the artefacts were imported from distant parts of north-west Europe; this is particularly true in the case of coins. Objects made of pewter, however, seem to have been locally produced. One deposit of unfinished artefacts was found in a Swedish lake. Although this has been explained in mundane terms, the fact that similar locations were being used for votive deposits suggests that metal production could also have been undertaken in special places and may have been attended by rituals (Zachrisson 1984: Chapter 3). It seems as if some of the artefacts were used to decorate organic objects, including wooden figures, antlers and drums. Among the other items found in votive deposits are iron arrowheads of exceptional quality (Mulk 1996). These may have been sacrificed at the conclusion of a particularly successful hunt. I shall return to the significance of some of the metal finds in Chapter 4.

Why were these sacrifices undertaken? There seem to have been a number of reasons, but all of them were closely bound up with the daily lives of the Saami. One of the main purposes of sacrifice was to ensure a dependable food supply. Thus offerings were made to the divine masters of the animals and to the supernatural rulers of different regions of the landscape. This was done in order to obtain an abundance of reindeer, fish and birds. The offerings were also intended

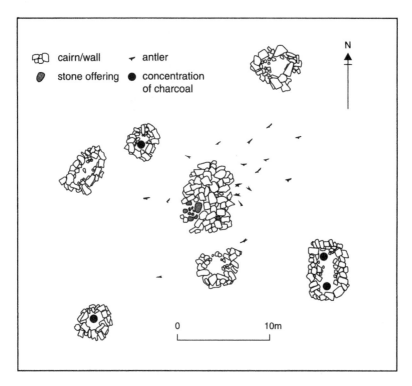

Figure 4 Detailed plan of the Saami sacrificial site at Grythaugen, Varanger,
northern Norway
Source: Information from Vorren and Eriksen 1993

to protect the health and fertility of the reindeer and to avoid illnesses that
seemed to emanate from underground, for this was regarded as the domain of
the dead. The weather was important too, and other sacrifices were carried out to
protect against lightning and to ensure that there was sufficient rain to nourish
the grass and moss on which the animals depended for food. Other reasons for
undertaking sacrifice included the need to propitiate elemental forces like the sun,
the moon and the winds. It was also equally important to make offerings to the
dead, for otherwise they might draw the living to them prematurely (Rydving
1995).

The ritual cycle was closely integrated into the process of food production.
There was a great autumn festival which was linked to the slaughter of reindeer
at the end of November, and at this time fresh wooden idols were carved. This
was an important moment for carrying out sacrifice. The idols would be covered
with blood and grease and might then be buried. Other sacrifices took place
during the winter, when the offerings were buried beneath the snow together with

spruce twigs, and in summer when leaves and grass were placed under the sacred stones.

The Saami ritual calendar was based on the behaviour of the bear. Winter was defined by the period during which it hibernated, summer was when it reappeared, and the transitional phases were again celebrated by rituals. Each new cycle was inaugurated by the bear festival (Terebikhin 1993). Why was the bear so important? It was a sacred animal and was thought of as the 'dog of the gods'. It would be easy to imagine that this was due to its size and strength, but the fact that it shares certain features with human beings may be just as important. Bears are omnivorous, and Tim Ingold suggests that their tracks resemble human footprints:

> They are manifestly intelligent, and display very human-like bodily and facial expressions, even weeping when upset. Their sitting position resembles that of a man, and so does their capacity to stand erect on their hind legs. Almost without exception, observers have noted the remarkably human form and proportions of the bear's carcass after it has been skinned, lending credence to the idea that the animal is really a man in disguise.
>
> (Ingold 1986: 257–8)

That may be why it was so important to retain the bones after the bear had been eaten and to bury them in the correct anatomical order. After the meal was over, its skin would be spread against a tree stump. The women of the community would be blindfolded and would fire arrows at the effigy (Mulk 1996).

On one level, the indigenous peoples of the Arctic took a practical attitude to the supernatural, harnessing its powers to increase the food supply. They also made a very distinctive use of the landscape, and imbued certain features of the terrain with supernatural properties. A few of these locations might be elaborated by small-scale timber or stone constructions, but in no sense did they effect a radical transformation of these places.

This level of analysis treats these different sites individually, but for the people who used them they would have been only the outward embodiment of a wider system of belief that had profound consequences for the ways in which the landscape was perceived. These sacred sites also played a part in people's understanding of how the world was formed and of their place within it.

Several elements seem to be especially important in such wider schemes. Communities in Arctic Europe made a vital distinction between this world, an underworld and the sky, and this seems to be illustrated by the imagery found on the Saami drum (Mulk 1994 and 1996; Rydving 1995). Particular places were especially important in allowing communication between these different domains; others took on a special significance by virtue of their geographical location. As part of this wider scheme, certain directions also assumed a special significance. As Yates (1987) has shown, some of these considerations even extended to the domestic sphere, where they were expressed in the organisation of space inside the Saami tent. For its occupants, this was the centre of the ritual cosmos, which moved with them whenever the structure was relocated.

The threefold division of the cosmos is a particular feature of this system. The world was created in horizontal layers: sky, earth and the underworld, each with its own gods, goddesses and ancestral spirits (Terebikhin 1993). The highest point in this system was the Pole Star. These three spheres correspond to the air, land and water and to the forest, the tundra and the sea respectively. They are connected to one another by a 'cosmic river', which sometimes takes the form of a tree, and on the Saami drum seems to be represented by a pillar or by a drawing of the sun.

The underworld was sometimes seen as the mirror image of the mundane world, and that may be why in so many cases the wooden idol was made from the bole of a tree that had been inverted so that the roots were uppermost. As in many other societies, the underworld is associated with the dead. Again, this reversed the features of the mundane world, and thus the feet of the dead, who must walk upside down, touch those of the living, who stand upright (Ingold 1986: 246). The places where rivers meet the sea may be among the locations that provide access to that underworld. They may be marked by rapids and by islands that are visited by shamans (Tilley 1991a: 130–3). These different levels have their own associations, and these may be reflected by the character of the different idols found at the sacrificial sites: the underworld was associated with fish; the everyday world was symbolised by the reindeer; whilst birds were obviously associated with the sky. In certain cases other creatures were drawn into this scheme, so that the fish might be replaced by wolves and the birds by bears (Terebikhin 1993).

The three layers of the cosmos may be reflected in the subdivision of time between summer, winter and the transitional periods represented by the bear festivals. Terebikhin (1993) has suggested that these divisions had still further ramifications. For him, these three periods are directly related to the three layers of the Saami cosmos. During the winter, women are associated with the lower world and with fishing; just as they are excluded from the sacrifices, they are not allowed to have any contact with the breeding of reindeer. In the ordinary world of the tundra, the men are associated with the reindeer in the summer, but in the winter they hunt wild animals that are linked with the forest (and, as we have seen, Terebikhin connects the forest with the celestial world). In Saami belief, female fishing is associated with the beginning of the world. Male hunting, on the other hand, brings about its end: 'The myth and ritual of fishing reproduced the process of the creation of the universe; ... the myth and ritual of cosmic hunting described the process of its disintegration' (Terebikhin 1993: 6)

Similar distinctions apply to the cosmic river, which runs from east to west. This is especially important as the west is associated with the position of the underworld. East represents life and the sunrise, and west stands for the sunset and death. North and south assume a rather different significance, for these directions are related to important distinctions within Saami society. In this case the north is linked with the sacred, with men, wild animals and with winter. The south, on the other hand, is connected with the profane, with women, domesticates and with the summer months (Yates 1987).

The sacrificial sites play an obvious part in this scheme, for they are in liminal locations at the edges of these different worlds. As we have seen, they were a male domain from which women were excluded, and they occur at the margins of lakes or on islands where the land meets the sea. They were placed on top of rocks, or on hills and mountains where the earth joins the heavens, and they were dedicated to the divinities associated with the forces of nature (Manker 1957). They are the components of a mythological landscape quite different to that encountered by field archaeology.

Return to Ukonsaari

Perhaps it is now a little clearer why I chose to begin this book with the early career of Arthur Evans. His work at Ukonsaari, limited as it was, had certain unfamiliar aspects for someone brought up on the archaeology of western Europe. Ukonsaari is, undoubtedly, one of the sacrificial sites of the indigenous population of northern Finland, but in a sense it must have fulfilled some of the roles played by monuments in other parts of the continent. It is not alone in this respect. One of the important lessons of studying Saami archaeology and eth-nography is that theirs is a landscape in which monuments play very little role. Indeed, those that were built have a limited distribution and a history that may not cover the entire period represented by the sacrificial sites (Poul Simonsen pers. comm.).

Instead of formally constituted monuments of the kind that have dominated the landscapes of prehistoric Europe, Arctic archaeology is concerned with the significance of unaltered places. In the case of the Saami, it is possible to specify some of the physical characteristics of the locations that were chosen, and also to identify a number of the processes that took place there. These were unusual features of the natural topography – features that stood out from the surrounding country, some of which recalled petrified people and animals – but they are even more important because we know a certain amount about their significance in Saami cosmology. The stones and other features that were selected from the wider terrain were credited with special powers and allowed contact with the super-natural. Those contacts were made through sacrifices that were entirely inte-grated into the daily lives of the Saami. At the same time, these places were only the visible signs of a complex cosmological scheme that involved three different worlds. These came into contact at natural locations such as caves and mountains.

It is only in the Arctic that there may be any chance of connecting European ethnography with the evidence of prehistoric and early historic archaeology, yet it seems somehow perverse that the landscape studies practised in the same contin-ent should be more closely influenced by accounts of Australia or America (for instance Carmichael et al. 1994; Nash 1997; Tilley 1994). This is one case in which European prehistorians can study the integration of traditional knowledge and beliefs about the landscape with the results of field archaeology. It provides a vital reminder of what they may be losing if they limit themselves to the significance of monuments. In that sense, the archaeology of Finland, Norway and Sweden offers a challenge to workers in other areas: how far is it possible to study the ancient landscape when the monuments are stripped away? That is one of the issues investigated here.

What follows

The book is divided into three parts, entitled 'Introductions', 'Explorations' and 'Interpretations' respectively, and Figure 5 locates the regions of Europe referred to, by chapter. The first part sets the scene. We have followed the young Arthur Evans to Ukonsaari already, and Chapter 2 continues his travels with his arrival in Crete two decades later, where he found more sacred caves. He contributed significantly to their interpretation before going on to investigate the palace at Knossos, the work for which he is best known today. This chapter reflects on the striking similarities between the use made of natural places in Finland and Crete, before turning to the writings of another traveller, Pausanias, who visited the sacred sites of Classical Greece in the second century AD. His *Periegesis* (*Guide to Greece*) provides the ideal counterpoint to Evans's journeys, for again he was able to draw on memories of a living tradition. Pausanias's writings shed remarkable light on the ways in which certain features of the topography were accorded a special significance and the manner in which they were used. So striking are the similarities between Finland, Crete and Greece, in fact, that they pose a special kind of problem. Why should such different societies have so much in common when one of them was egalitarian and the others were early states? One answer may be provided by Eliade's (1954, 1964) studies of comparative religion, with their emphasis on an overarching cosmology. Another approach may be to consider the common features that are experienced in a state of religious ecstasy and the purely physiological reasons why these should be found.

Chapter 3 concludes the introductory section of the book by considering changing perceptions of the landscape over time. It also discusses what is meant by 'natural' places. It isolates four elements that seem to be shared by the different accounts summarised in Chapters 1 and 2, each of which is amenable to investigation by archaeological methods. They are: the provision of votive offerings; the presence of 'art' at natural places in the landscape; the use of special locations as production sites; and the recreation of a small number of ritually important locations as conventional monuments. Each topic has been studied in its own right and according to a different kind of agenda. It appears useful to bring them together here.

Part 2 provides a more detailed analysis of each of these elements and its potential contribution to an archaeology of natural places. In each case the starting point is one of the ethnographic cases considered earlier. Alternating chapters take their point of departure from these examples. Thus my discussions of votive

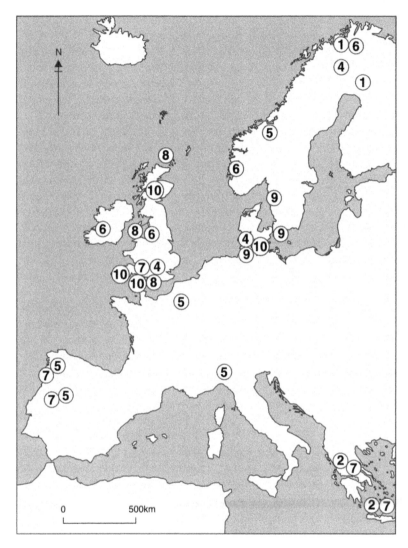

Figure 5 Map showing the regions of Europe studied in the text; the numbers
are those of individual chapters in the book

offerings and production sites build on some of the lessons to be learnt from
Arctic archaeology, whilst the studies of art and monument building develop out
of the prehistory of the Mediterranean. Although these come from opposite ends
of Europe, the archaeological cases range even more widely. To some extent, the
effect of these is intended to be cumulative, so that each can build on some of the
possibilities suggested by its predecessors. Thus Chapter 4 considers the hoards

and votive deposits of Neolithic and Bronze Age Europe in the light of what we can learn from the sacrificial sites of the Saami, and Chapter 5 is an account of prehistoric rock art which develops from Pausanias's description of the altars found on isolated mountain tops in Greece. Chapter 6 returns to Scandinavia and embarks on a detailed discussion of the relationship between stone axe quarries and a number of major groups of rock art, whilst Chapter 7 comes back to Arthur Evans's work on Crete and begins with a more detailed account of the sacred caves that he found there and their translation into stone-built monuments.

Each of the four chapters that form Part 2 is also illustrated by at least one archaeological case study. Thus Chapter 4 concludes with an account of the bog hoards of Neolithic Denmark, and Chapter 5 makes a detailed comparison between neighbouring styles of rock art and their relationship to the landscape in two areas of Europe, one from Iberia and the other from Norway. Chapter 6 leads from a discussion of stone axe production into a new study of the significance of the bluestones at Stonehenge. In the same way, Chapter 7 concludes with an account of how the different elements found in the rock art of northern Portugal were brought together in the construction of sanctuaries and tombs. Each of these monuments came to encapsulate the features of the wider landscape in that region.

Part 3 brings all these elements together and integrates them with some of the ideas discussed in the opening section of the book. Two chapters provide regional case studies, whilst the final chapter, which also sums up the findings of this project, covers a longer period of time and is an interpretation of practices that occurred over an altogether wider area. Chapter 8 studies the landscape of the British Neolithic, showing how its different elements were articulated with the massive public monuments that have for so long been the major focus of research. It seeks to relate these to their wider contexts in the prehistoric landscape, and does so using evidence from Wessex. It considers votive deposits and production sites, and suggests that both these elements were brought together in an archi- tectural setting. Here the emphasis is on the ways in which they might be used to frame a narrative concerned with origins, places and the role of people in the world.

Chapter 9 is primarily about the Bronze Age archaeology of Scandinavia. Here the main focus is on the relationship between monuments and rock carvings, but in this case the basic interpretation is a very different one. Instead of investigating structured deposits, it is concerned mainly with the images found on the carved surfaces and their distribution in relation to other components of the landscape. In this case, the discussion extends to questions of cosmology, and seeks to relate each of these different elements to a wider perception of the world that may have had its origins amongst northern hunter gatherers. This interpretation operates on several different levels, from the distribution of archaeological material about the ancient landscape to the organisation of individual panels of rock art, and from the imagery carved on natural outcrops to that found on Bronze Age metalwork.

The book concludes with a more general review of the changing significance of natural places in the prehistoric and early medieval landscapes of northern and western Europe. Its point of departure is Tilley's idea that Neolithic monuments took over the significance of important places in the landscape and brought them under control. This idea has something to be said for it, but the process was more protracted than he suggests. Chapter 10 shows how the creation of monuments led to the emergence of a new generation of significant natural places, and how these were assimilated into the political process. Rather than this development taking place over the Neolithic period, it extended into the Early Middle Ages. The closing section of the book reflects on the significance of natural places for studies of the ancient landscape and the changing relationships between them and the world of human constructions.

This takes us a long way from the cave of thunder, but Ukonsaari is as good a place as any to begin what will be a long and complicated journey. The career of Arthur Evans provides a connecting link with what follows in Chapter 2; after that, we have to find our own path. The questions that we need to consider are of interest outside archaeology, but the ethnographic evidence soon runs out. If they can be answered at all, it will be by archaeology alone.

Overworlds and underworlds

Sacred places in a Classical landscape

This chapter considers the later career of Arthur Evans when he worked on Crete, where once again natural places took on a special significance. It reflects on their importance in Minoan archaeology, before turning to the work of another traveller, Pausanias. In the second century AD he attempted to recreate the sacred landscape of Classical Greece by studying the surviving remains of temples and shrines and setting down the beliefs associated with them. Among the places described in his *Guide to Greece* were a considerable number of natural features. This chapter summarises that evidence and considers how it is interpreted today. There are striking similarities between the kinds of locations accorded a special significance in the Classical world and those used by mobile populations in the Arctic. This chapter considers these similarities and suggests some of the ways in which they might be studied.

Introduction

Twenty-one years after his visit to Finland, Arthur Evans was travelling again (Brown 1993: 37–84; Evans 1943). He had become the director of a university museum and had a definite agenda in mind: he intended to carry out archaeological fieldwork in Crete. Above all, he was interested in investigating an ancient system of writing, and wished to acquire artefacts for his collection. Although his main objective was Knossos, he visited many other sites before he was able to work there. As he journeyed about the island, history seems to have repeated itself, for, time and again, he was drawn to caves and rock shelters that contained unusual deposits of artefacts. Before he could devote his energies to the study of monumental architecture, he became involved in what I call the archaeology of natural places.

Evans's travels around the island made him acutely aware of the large number of caves, rock shelters and mountain tops that seemed to be associated with finds of distinctive artefacts, particularly figurines. They did not seem to provide evidence of everyday life, yet some of these locations were within sight of the Minoan palaces that claimed his attention in later years. On his first visit to Crete, in 1893, he purchased metalwork from a cave near Patsos and visited the Kamares

Cave, which had produced Minoan pottery. Two years later, he was in Crete again and his travels took him to a sacred cave above Psychro which was considered to be the birthplace of Zeus. This site was associated with more figures of humans and animals. He returned to Crete a year later and excavated at the Psychro Cave, where he identified a stone offering table. He also investigated a rock shelter that he had seen two years before. Finally, in 1899, he made plans for a fuller excavation at the cult centre in the Psychro Cave which was to be conducted by a colleague (Figure 6). By 1900, when he began work at Knossos, Evans had laid the foundations for modern investigations of the caves and peak sanctuaries of Crete.

By this stage in his career, Evans had encountered a similar phenomenon in the archaeology of two quite different cultures. In each case there was convincing evidence for the deposition of specialised offerings at natural features in the landscape. What is so striking about them is that they were created by very different societies. In Finland, the sacred cave at Ukonsaari had been used by hunters or reindeer herders, whilst the distinctive deposits that caught his attention in Crete spanned the early development of the state. Even there, however, Evans was investigating a society whose beliefs were largely undocumented.

Before he began his excavations at Knossos, Arthur Evans investigated a number of prehistoric cave sanctuaries in Crete. As we have seen, they were characterised by a particular set of artefacts, including figurines. At one level, these sites

Figure 6 The Psychro Cave at the time of its excavation in 1900
Source: Photograph reproduced by permission of the Ashmolean Museum, Oxford

played an important role in the evolution of prehistoric society on the island, but, at another, they formed part of a more general pattern in Mediterranean archaeology. Caves, rock shelters and mountain peaks assumed a similar significance in many different areas, extending through Greece and Italy as far west as Spain (Alcock and Osborne 1994; Edlund 1987; Simon 1992). Their interpretation poses certain problems. Although many of these places were used by people who left accounts of their religious practices, these sources have all too little to say about the topography of ancient belief. It is difficult to integrate them with the evidence on the ground in the way that has been possible in the Arctic. Fortunately, there is a case in which archaeology and ethnography can still be brought together. This is the work of Pausanias.

A guide to *A Guide to Greece*

Pausanias was a doctor who wrote his *Periegesis* or *Guide to Greece* in the second century AD (Arafat 1996; Elsner 1995: Chapter 4; Habicht 1985). He was a member of 'a circle of almost professional antiquaries' (Levi 1971: 2), and in one sense he was both a historian of religion and the first field archaeologist, describing the sites of Classical antiquity when many of their remains still survived. On the other hand, he was not concerned with minute documentation, as a modern researcher might be. He was asserting the value of Greek culture under Roman imperial rule, and he was writing a guide for travellers. He was also recovering

> a sacred landscape that was the main vehicle for the display and expression of social and religious monuments, customs and ideologies that belonged to an otherwise irretrievable past. Pausanias wrote as a native inhabitant of a notional land, so to speak, which nonetheless could be made real by attaching explanations and stories to particular sites, monuments and natural features.
>
> (Birge 1994: 231)

That reference to natural features is especially important, for it raises some of the issues that I have already identified in the early career of Arthur Evans.

For our purposes, the work of Pausanias provides the ideal counterpoint to Evans's travels and does so for one simple reason. Evans was identifying places that had been associated with distinctive groups of artefacts, and was trying to work out ways of interpreting them. By concentrating on the topography of these places, he was able to identify a group of unusual sites, and through his studies of the distinctive assemblages found there he strengthened their interpretation as sanctuaries. In both respects these places were outside the sphere of domestic life. Pausanias, on the other hand, was studying the last traces of a living tradition. He had the artefacts, chiefly sculptures, to hand, and visited these places himself, but he was also able to draw on what was still remembered of their religious significance. In that respect he had some access to their original meanings. A number of these places remained in use, and he could learn about others from his informants. We can sum up these contrasts by saying that Evans's work follows the principles of modern field archaeology, whilst Pausanias's account is closer to ethnography.

Even so, the *Guide to Greece* has its limitations. Pausanias took a rather romantic view of the past and was most interested in the early history of these places. He laid greater emphasis on their Classical origins than their use during the Roman period, when he himself was writing. He was a connoisseur of ancient statuary, and wrote more about the surviving sculptures on these sites than he did about their other characteristics (Habicht 1985). Nor is it always clear whether he was describing natural places that had developed into monuments, or locations that had remained entirely unaltered. Even so, his account is extremely informative.

Two extracts from the *Guide to Greece* will serve to illustrate the character of his work and its relevance to an archaeology of natural places. The first treats the evidence at a very general level. Describing the sacred landscape of Attica, Pausanias writes:

> On the . . . mountains are images of the gods. On Pentelicus there is an image of Athena, on Hymettus an image of Hymettian Zeus; and there are altars of Showery Zeus and Foreseeing Apollo. On Parnes is a bronze image of Parnethian Zeus, and an altar of Sign-giving Zeus. There is another altar on Parnes, on which they sacrifice, invoking Zeus now as the Showery god, now as the Averter of Ills. There is a small mountain called Anchesmus, with an image of Anchesmian Zeus.
>
> (Pausanias 1898, Book 1: 32. 2)

In this case, it is clear that significant places in the landscape – locations that recall the siting of Evans's sanctuaries on Crete – had been embellished by sculptures dedicated to the gods, but there is nothing in his text to indicate that buildings had been erected there. Sometimes these places had stories associated with them, so that they played their part in a mythical narrative.

My second extract accounts for the origin of a river:

> In the territory of Haliartus there is a river Lophis. It is said that the district being originally parched and waterless, one of the rulers went to Delphi and inquired how they should find water in the land. The Pythian priestess commanded him to slay the first person he should meet on his return to Haliartus. On his arrival he was met by his son Lophis, and, without hesitation, he struck the young man with his sword. The youth had life enough left to run about, and where the blood flowed water gushed from the ground. Therefore the river is called Lophis.
>
> (Pausanias 1898, Book 9: 33. 3)

It would be all too easy to multiply examples of Pausanias's accounts of individual places, but for our purposes it is more important to consider his testimony as a whole. Which locations did he single out as having a special significance in the sacred landscape of Greece? Were there clear preferences for certain kinds of places rather than others? And how many of those features are of types that could be recognised today?

The ten books of the *Periegesis* can be treated together for this purpose, although they describe different areas of Greece (Figure 7). Despite the difficulties of distinguishing between monuments and unaltered features of the landscape, certain consistent patterns can be traced throughout the text. Perhaps the commonest feature to be ascribed a sacred character was the spring, although in most cases the spring itself might provide the focus for a group of buildings. Much the same significance was attached to three other locations: mountains, caves and trees; many of the latter were found in groves, although individual examples could

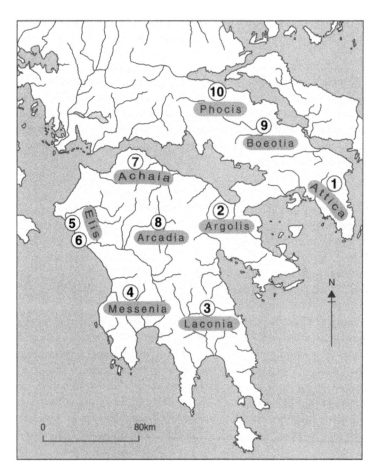

Figure 7 The regions described in Pausanias's *Periegesis*; the numbers refer
to the separate books that compose this work

assume a sacred identity in their own right (Birge 1994). Again there are problems in reading Pausanias's text. Some of the groves were associated with stone buildings, similar structures could be erected on sacred mountains, and some of the caves were associated with other groups of monuments, yet in each case it seems as if the natural features of these places were their most important characteristic. Apart from the woods, groves and trees, these are components of the landscape that can still be identified today (Figure 8).

The same applies to a number of other sites that were accorded a special significance in Pausanias's account of Classical Greece. They may have been less numerous than those mentioned already, or they may have attracted less interest during his travels. These include gorges, rocks, rivers, lakes and waterfalls. On the coast, a similar significance extended to capes and small islands. Once again, these are mainly features of the landscape that survive to the present day. It is interesting that the same kinds of places assumed a sacred character in the Greek colonies in Italy. According to Edlund's study *The Gods and the Place*, these were mountains, promontories, caves, trees, groves, lakes, rivers, springs and the sea (Edlund 1987).

How were these places used? The deposits found in the major Classical sanctuaries have been studied by archaeologists for many years (Linders and Nordquist 1987), and include a range of votive deposits that recall the offerings identified by Arthur Evans in Crete, although they also include weaponry, exotic materials and

Figure 8 The sacred landscape of Classical Greece: an early twentieth-century photograph of the view from the sanctuary at Delphi
Source: Poulsen 1920

a variety of elaborate artefacts dedicated to the gods. It is worth comparing these well-known assemblages with the simpler practices that Pausanias describes at two entirely natural locations in Greece, Plataia and Patrai.

Near Plataia, where the local people held a festival:

> there is an oak wood . . . ; the trunks of the oak-trees are the largest in Boeotia. To this wood come the Plataeans [who] set out pieces of boiled flesh and keep a sharp watch on the crows, which come flocking to them; the other birds do not trouble them in the least. They observe the crow which pounces on the flesh and the tree on which he perches. Then they fell the tree on which he perched, and make the *daedalum* [a wooden image] out of it . . . . Having decked the image . . . and having set it up on a wagon, they place a bridesmaid on the wagon . . . . Then they drive the wagon from the river to the top of Cithaeron. On the summit of the mountain an altar has been got ready. They make it in this fashion – they put together quadrangular blocks of wood, fitting them into each other, just in the same way as if they were constructing an edifice of stone. Then, having raised it to a height, they pile brushwood on it. The cities and magistrates sacrifice each a cow to Hera and a bull to Zeus, and burn the victims, which are filled with wine and incense, together with the images on the altar. . . . I know of no flame that rises so high, and is seen so far.
>
> (Pausanias 1898, Book 9: 3. 4)

That example combines two of the commonest elements: the use of trees and the significance accorded to prominent mountain peaks. A second passage extends to the use of watery locations, although Pausanias makes an explicit comparison between these and another kind of site:

> The water of Ino . . . is as big as a small lake, but much deeper. At the festival of Ino they throw barley loaves into this water. If the water takes and keeps the loaves, it is a good augury for the person who threw them in; but if it sends them up to the surface, it is judged a bad omen. The craters at Etna give like indications. For people cast vessels of gold and silver and all sorts of victims into them; and if the fire swallows them up the people are glad, taking it for a happy omen; but if the flame rejects what a man has thrown into it they think evil will befall that man.
>
> (Pausanias 1898, Book 3: 23. 5)

On other occasions, the most important element was that the sacrifices themselves should come from the natural world. They should not be domesticates. Pausanias provides an extraordinary account of this practice at Patrai:

> Every year the Patreans hold a festival called the Laphria in honour of Artemis, at which they have a peculiar mode of sacrifice. Round the altar in a

circle they set up green logs of wood . . . and inside this fence they pile the driest wood on the altar. When the time of the festival is at hand they construct a smooth ascent to the altar by heaping earth on the altar steps. The festival opens with a gorgeous procession in honour of Artemis, the rear being brought up by the virgin priestess riding on a car drawn by deer . . . . The people bring the edible kinds of birds and victims of every sort, and throw them alive on the altar; also wild boars, deer, and roe; others bring the cubs of wolves and bears, others the full-grown beasts. They also lay on the altar the fruit of cultivated trees. Next they set fire to the wood. I have seen a bear and other beasts struggling to get out at the first burst of the flames, and some of them actually escaping by sheer strength. But the people who threw them in drag them back again to the burning pyre. They do not remember that any one was ever wounded by the beasts.

(Pausanias 1898, Book 7: 18. 7)

Such practices were very varied. In the first extract, wooden images were carried in procession from the town to the countryside and were sacrificed along with animals on a mountain top. In the second, offerings of food and valuables were cast into the depths of a lake or into the crater of a volcano, and in the third passage the sacrifice consisted entirely of wild animals and fruits. In this case it took place at an altar surrounded by an enormous pyre. Other sacred places seem to have been located at the apparent edges of the world: on the coast, on offshore islands and in mountain passes. Pausanias's reconstruction emphasises the springs where the water rises from the earth below, for the *Periegesis* is much concerned with underground streams and rivers. This account of the sacred geography of Classical Greece returns time and again to the importance of the caves that link the outer world to what lies beneath its surface (Figure 9).

The lessons of Pausanias

Chapter 1 described some of the most striking features of Saami ethnography in relation to the archaeological material found at their sacrificial sites, but, with minor exceptions, that account was concerned with a landscape that did not contain any monuments. The writings of Pausanias are important because they illustrate the significance of natural features even at a time when monumental architecture had assumed a vital role.

The work of Vincent Scully (1962) is particularly relevant here. Before this kind of study became so fashionable in Classical archaeology, he suggested that there was a significant relationship between the physical configuration of the places where temples and sanctuaries were built and the gods to whom they were dedicated. That interpretation might seem too impressionistic to carry much weight, but there is some evidence that certain kinds of locations were associated with the appropriate deities. Jost has emphasised that in Arcadia:

Figure 9 The sacred landscape of Greece according to
         Pausanias

> Particular divinities demand one sort of terrain rather than another. This is
> especially clearly marked in the case of plains liable to flooding. . . . In these
> areas Artemis, the goddess associated with dampness, and Poseidon, the mas-
> ter of underground waters, are particularly often found. . . . Other parts of
> the plains and valleys are home to the cult of Demeter, goddess associated
> with the fertility of the soil and vegetation. . . . In the mountains, the deities
> to whom pastoralists address themselves are Artemis, goddess of border areas
> and of hunting, Hermes, honoured on Mount Kyllene as the rustic god of
> shepherds, and Pan, the divine goatherd and hunter.
>
> (Jost 1994, 220)

Other gods were associated with the towns. The effect was to extend divine
protection to the landscape as a whole.

   This is not just a matter of defining the jurisdiction of particular gods, for, like
the reindeer herders of the Arctic, the Classical Greeks had their own conception
of the cosmos. This is better known than that of the Saami, but both schemes
share certain features. Again the mundane world had its boundaries. Above it,
particular gods were associated with the mountain tops where the heavens met the

earth, and beneath its surface there was an underworld (Burkert 1985). This scheme is also reflected in the dedications of the sanctuaries, for these were the appropriate places for sacrifices to particular gods. Thus Zeus is particularly associated with sanctuaries on mountain tops. Approximately 100 cult sites of this character are documented. By contrast, the cave at Tainaron provided access to the underworld. Another cave led Aeneas to the domain of the dead. It may be no accident that in Greek mythology, as well as in Saami belief, the boundary between the living and the dead could be represented by a river.

The peculiar character of some of these places is emphasised by the ways in which people treated them. They were located outside the sphere of normal domestic life, and yet that very distinction was important. Thus there were cases in which domesticated animals had to be sacrificed at the sanctuaries rather than the game that could have been hunted in the vicinity. In other cases, all the offerings had to come from the wild, even if this involved some danger. Sometimes there was an explicit emphasis on role reversals (Buxton 1994: Chapter 6). Young girls might disguise themselves as bears, or mountain cult sites might be visited by people from the towns who had dressed as shepherds for the purpose in what has been described as 'a one-day ritual transhumance. The highest turn[ed] into the lowest, the most prominent citizens into shepherds, for this [was] the [sacred ground], where, in ritual as in myth, metamorphoses and reversals [took] place' (Buxton 1994: 94). The same applied to other cult sites, where women went to worship Dionysus. In daily life the mountains were associated with shepherds and hunters and many of them were places that were visited only by men, but here again the conventions of normal life were overturned.

The seashore was another marginal area associated with ritual activity. The sea provided food, but it also threatened human life. Unexpected discoveries could be made there, from the head of Orpheus to images of the gods and heroes, yet the coastline was also the place to offer sacrifices before undertaking a hazardous journey. Again it is worth quoting from Buxton's *Imaginary Greece*:

> In ritual, as in myth, contact with the sea can constitute a fresh beginning, a reinauguration of hope. In this connection it is worth emphasising the exact location of these rituals: the sea-*shore*. In the relatively tideless Mediterranean, the shore is narrow – a line, a boundary, a margin, a place where opposites meet. In cult, it is the site for the transition between polluted and pure. In myth, it is where the human meets the uncanny, . . . where the no-longer-human-but-not-properly-dead belong . . . and where the marginalised hero withdraws.
>
> (Buxton 1994: 102–3; emphasis in original)

The seashore is one edge of the settled land. Caves and springs are another, and they share the common characteristic that they are all places where the outer world communicates with the depths. As we have seen, both were treated in rather similar ways to the other cult centres considered here.

Rather than enumerate more examples of the uses that were made of individual sites, it is important to stress their common features. These places not only permitted communication between two different worlds, they also celebrated the relationship between quite different times. We have seen how Arthur Evans was shown the birthplace of Zeus at a cave in Crete, and it is remarkable how many places of the same character were associated with identical claims. Other caves were the places where monsters and heroes were born. Caves are often found in mountains, and mountains too were associated with origins. They were connected with an older race of heroes and with strange creatures, half men and half animals. They were the places where the first people had lived, and they may have been the only land that remained uncovered during a terrible flood (Buxton 1994: 81–96).

Because of these associations, the use of natural places may have involved a celebration of origins. At times, the connection is even more specific and even extended to a kind of re-enactment of history itself. This may provide another explanation for the sacrifices made on mountain tops by people dressed as herdsmen, and certainly seems to account for the offerings made to Demeter:

> At the cavern to which the violated Demeter withdrew, individuals and, annually, the whole community made offerings of grapes and other cultivated fruit, honeycombs and raw wool, products recalling a 'non-cereal' existence.
> (Buxton 1994: 107)

Again the ritual seems to have involved an explicit reference to the earlier history of the community.

In the mind's eye

It is remarkable how many similarities exist between the situations described so far. These extend some way beyond the types of places that were accorded a special significance in the past, for, in each case, particular locations were associated with particular divinities and allowed the population to come into contact with the supernatural. This remains the case whether that location was a shaman's island in the rapids of a Scandinavian river or the oracle's cave in a sanctuary on a Greek mountain. Those rituals may have re-enacted the processes by which the world was made, and they may also have permitted communication between quite different domains. Indeed, one feature that both areas share in common is the importance of caves and the seashore.

Ethnographic studies, not unlike those quoted already, show that many features of the landscape might have special powers. They could play their part in a mythical narrative and their significance might well be interpreted and reinterpreted from one generation to the next. Places that were left entirely unmodified might be among the most significant to the people who visited them: rivers could assume special properties; the paths crossing the landscape recreated the movements of the ancestors; and entire areas of the country might take on a sacred character (Bender 1993; Carmichael *et al.* 1994; Hirsch and O'Hanlon 1995; Ucko and Layton 1999). Such information could be lost to field archaeology, even though it plays a critical role in defining land rights in the present. The everyday landscape that offers food and shelter for those who live there might also provide a means of interpreting the world.

How have these topics been explored? One way of investigating these connections is through the literature of comparative religion, and in particular the widely quoted work of the Romanian scholar Mircea Eliade (1954 and 1964). Eliade considers that all religions contain two competing principles: cosmos and chaos. Cosmos is the domain of human order and, by extension, that of sacred power, whilst chaos is its opposite and stands for the profane. The two elements exist in tension, and the principle of order must be reasserted constantly. Religious practices provide one way of mediating between those two extremes. Communication is all-important here: it must happen in special locations where the sacred world is revealed. These are known as 'hierophanies': literally, places where the sacred world shows itself. Eliade's example seems peculiarly appropriate to an archaeology of natural places:

> The object appears as a receptacle of an exterior force that differentiates it from its milieu and gives it meaning and value. This force may reside in the substance of the object or in its form: a rock reveals itself to be sacred because its very existence is an hierophany: incompressible, invulnerable, it is that which man is not. It resists time. . . . Take the commonest of stones; it will be raised to the ranks of 'precious', that is impregnated with a magical or religious power by virtue of its symbolic shape or its origin: thunder stone, held to have fallen from the sky; pearl because it comes from the depths of the sea.
>
> (Eliade 1954: 4)

Several features are particularly interesting here. The choice of sacred stones for their distinctive shape immediately recalls the sacrificial places of the Saami, whilst the reference to rocks associated with the earth and the sea introduces another fundamental aspect of Eliade's scheme. The sacred centre is where different cosmic levels come into contact: the earth, the sky and the underworld. They are locations where communication between these spheres is possible. In Eliade's scheme, for example, 'the Sacred Mountain – where heaven and earth meet – [is] situated at the centre of the world' (1954: 12). They are connected by what he defines as the *axis mundi*, which joins these elements together and allows communication between them.

Thus religious experience is balanced between cosmos and chaos, the sacred and the profane, the ordered and the uncontrolled. Human life takes place in between two other worlds, in Eliade's terms heaven and hell, and among the places where sacred powers manifest themselves are those features of the landscape where all three come closest together. They might include caves and rock fissures that communicate with the world below, and the trees and mountains that rise into the sky. These are among the elements that are fundamental to the maintenance of order, and for that reason they have to be treated with special care. Ceremonies carried out in these locations play a particularly important part in maintaining order in the human world and in averting the threat of chaos (Eliade 1964).

At first sight this scheme might account for the similarities between the two examples that have been considered here. There is the same emphasis on special-ised locations, on overworlds and underworlds, the areas of the landscape where fundamentally different elements meet. Despite these similarities, however, there are certain dangers in taking such an approach. Eliade's interpretation is one that treats the 'sacred' as a category that cannot be analysed: it must be accepted on its own terms (Lawson and McCauley 1990: 13). At the same time, it is a model that is extraordinarily generalised, for it is based less on a systematic analysis than on cross-cultural generalisation of an extravagant kind. In that respect it has exactly the same weakness as processual archaeology. His reconstruction is built out of elements taken from many different cultures and systems of belief, and in his commitment to a single powerful model Eliade overrides the details of local practices and beliefs. Archaeologists claim to have turned their back on reconstructions of the past based on piecemeal comparisons with living societies, but in seeking to extend the range of landscape studies they could place too much emphasis on models of this kind. In doing so, they may lose sight of the specific evidence that they are trying to interpret.

Many of the elements that are shared by the different areas considered here are common features of ecstatic religions. This has tended to be overlooked because of current controversies over the correct use of the term 'shamanism'. Like any anthropological concept couched in the language of the people being studied, there is a danger of extending this notion too far. Nevertheless, certain practices are widely shared, however we choose to describe them. Ian Lewis quotes the definition provided by the Russian scholar Basilov:

> a cult whose central axis is the belief in the ability of some individuals chosen by some spirits to communicate with them while in a state of ecstasy and perform the functions of an intermediary between the world of spirits and the human collectivity.

> (Lewis 1986: 92)

Lewis then adds that

> it does not matter how the balance between possession and soul-flight is pitched, whether or not a three-tier cosmology is present (though it often is) or whether [the] . . . cosmic tree is part of the picture (though it often is). These and many other symbolic motifs are widely if not universally associ-ated with shamanism.

> (Ibid.)

For our purposes, the most important feature of ecstatic religion is the way in which particular people enter a state of possession or trance and may seem to travel to other places and times. They can experience the sensation of swimming or flying and may pass through the surface of the earth or rise into the air. Sometimes they can see into the future or contact the dead. The subtitle of one of the chapters in Eliade's account of shamanism sums up the situation very well: 'Celestial ascents. Descents to the underworld' (Eliade 1964: Chapter 6).

It follows that it is possible to talk of a shamanic cosmology, for this is the way in which the world is perceived during altered states of consciousness (Figure 10). The elements are those considered by Eliade to be fundamental to religious experience:

> The pre-eminently shamanic technique is the passage from one cosmic region to another – from earth to the sky or from earth to the underworld. The shaman knows the mystery of the break-through in place. This communication among the cosmic zones is made possible by the very structure of the universe. . . . The universe in general is conceived as having three levels – sky, earth, underworld – connected by a central axis. . . . The essential scheme is always to be seen; there are three great cosmic regions which can be successively transversed because they are linked together by a central axis. This axis, of course, passes through an 'opening,' a 'hole': it is through this hole that the soul of the shaman in ecstasy can fly up or down in the course of his celestial or infernal journeys.
>
> (Eliade 1964: 259)

Although the subtitle of Eliade's account of shamanism is *Archaic Techniques of Ecstasy*, the book does not account for these sensations. That is because Eliade is

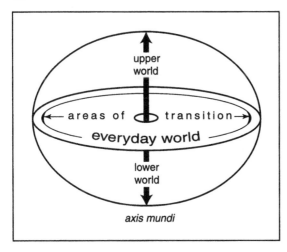

Figure 10 Sacred cosmology according to Mircea Eliade

concerned with religious practice. More recent research has suggested that these feelings have their origin in the human nervous system. They result from a wide variety of different stimuli – Eliade's 'techniques' – and it is because all human beings share the same physical properties that they undergo rather similar experiences under these conditions:

> Time-honoured techniques include the use of alcoholic spirits, hypnotic suggestion, rapid over-breathing, the inhalation of smoke and vapours, music and dancing; and the ingestion of . . . drugs. . . . Even without these aids, much the same effects can be produced, although usually . . . more slowly, by such self-inflicted or externally imposed mortifications and privations as fasting and ascetic contemplation. . . . The inspirational effect of sensory deprivation, implied in the stereotyped mystical 'flight' into the wilderness, has also been well documented in laboratory experiments. The most exciting scientific discoveries, here, are surely those of . . . natural opiates in the human brain . . . whose release is promoted by such traditional methods of trance induction.
>
> (Lewis 1989: 34)

Of course, these physical impressions are interpreted in terms of local understandings of the world, and that is why shamanic practice is apparently so varied. At the same time, the shamanic universe postulated by Eliade is simply his interpretation of a variety of rather similar experiences reported by ritual specialists in different parts of the world (Vitebsky 1995). The fact that similar ideas are found in quite different societies says very little about the nature of religious revelation. Rather, it describes a set of experiences rooted in nothing more arcane than the nervous system.

These shamanic experiences are important for our purposes because these sensations may become associated with particular kinds of location in the landscape. Eliade writes of 'holes' or 'openings', and this is an apt description of the caves and rock fissures that play such a major part in the sacred geography of both the Arctic and the Classical worlds. He discusses the sensation of flight, which is naturally associated with the trees and mountains that reach into the sky and with the birds that are found there. Shamans also describe the sensation of swimming underwater, and this provides an obvious explanation of the reasons why rivers, springs, lakes and even the sea are associated with the transition to another domain. Among the Saami the sea is associated with the dead, whilst for the Greeks the underworld was reached by crossing a river. The point is not to look for precise parallels between these cultures but to accept that in very different societies ecstatic experiences might become associated with similar features of the landscape.

Unfortunately, that is the beginning, not the end, of the story. Although it helps to show why particular kinds of places assumed a special significance in ancient societies, it does not explain how archaeologists can study them. That question is explored in Chapter 3.

Chapter 3

Nature study

The archaeological potential of unaltered places

There are problems in assuming that different ages perceive landscapes in the same ways, just as there are difficulties in treating the distinction between culture and nature as a universal. Even so, there are good reasons for suggesting that unaltered features of the landscape should be studied more systematically by archaeologists. In the light of the ethnographic accounts presented earlier, this chapter suggests four areas of enquiry: votive deposits, rock art, production sites and the relationship between monuments and features of the natural terrain. In the past each has been studied according to an entirely different agenda, but they could also contribute to a new form of landscape archaeology.

First principles

There are features of the landscape that have hardly changed over the centuries. The mountains remain undiminished, the rivers follow the same course and many of the caves still dominate the terrain. In one sense this is reassuring for archaeologists; in another, it is entirely deceptive. Although these features may retain the same form for long periods of time, the ways in which they are perceived are very likely to have altered. Thus different styles of landscape painting go in and out of fashion; different regions of the world attract visitors from one generation to another; and different societies put quite separate values on such features as mountains, forests and the coast. What became the English 'Lake District' was avoided until the eighteenth century because it seemed threatening and incoherent (Murdoch 1984). Then it was rediscovered and visited by tourists, writers and painters, until it achieved its apotheosis in the landscape mysticism of Wordsworth.

Other regions have experienced a similar transformation in public perceptions, but to say this is to project what is really a composite view. The reactions of local people can be very different to those of visitors, and the significance of particular locations may be contested between groups with different interests (Strang 1997). Individual reactions may vary even more sharply. A good example is provided by Gustave Flaubert, who took a holiday in the Alps in 1874 in order to calm his nerves. He did not respond to his new surroundings. As he wrote in a letter,

> I feel completely bored. . . . The Alps are out of all proportion to human existence. They are too big to be useful. This is the third time that they have provoked a disagreeable reaction in me and I hope that it's the last.
>
> (Beaumont 1985: 87)

The historian Keith Thomas has traced similar changes in attitudes to animals. In a little over 200 years, opinion shifted from the theological view that animals had been created by God specifically for human exploitation to a growing conviction that such exploitation could be harmful and morally wrong. Ideas shifted along with other changes in society. During the eighteenth century:

> The growth of towns led to a new longing for the countryside. The progress of cultivation had fostered a taste for weeds, mountains and unsubdued nature. The new-found security from wild animals had generated an increasing concern to protect birds and preserve wild creatures in their natural state.
>
> (Thomas 1983: 301)

As he shows, it is impossible to consider attitudes to the natural world without investigating how those ideas conformed to other areas of life.

In fact, the very concept of nature may be a specific feature of Western philosophy. Many writers, from Descartes to Lévi-Strauss, have contrasted what they call 'culture' and 'nature', yet neither term seems to have a universal application (Ellen 1996; Thomas 1996: Chapter 1). Nonetheless, human societies do need to impose some structure on their lives, and individual groups may chance on rather similar distinctions that are drawn from their own, essentially local experience. Thus the Saami find it useful to distinguish between the significance of wild and domesticated animals, for this mirrors a more basic contrast between the sacred and profane. This is also related to differences of gender and is expressed by the form of the dwellings in which they live. In the same way, the Greeks who offered sacrifices at some of the mountain sanctuaries distinguished between the domestic animals that they had brought with them and the wild animals that could be hunted closer to these sites. The contrasts between the mountains and the towns from which these people came were expressed by the different gods they venerated and in one case by the costumes that they wore. Worshippers dressed in fleeces to emphasise the difference between the life of the shepherd in the mountains and their own lives in the towns. We should not abandon the distinction between culture and nature where it is still useful. On the other hand, we should not rely upon it unless there are good reasons for doing so.

It follows that if we are to investigate the archaeology of 'natural' places, we must be careful how we characterise them. Perhaps the most satisfactory way of proceeding is to identify a series of recurrent features. This discussion draws on the ethnographic examples employed in Chapters 1 and 2.

'Natural' places are not monuments, because they have not been constructed by human labour. Their form has not experienced any significant modification over time. That is not to say that later generations may understand them in this way. As the examples quoted in the previous chapter show, they may explain their genesis in mythological terms: these places could have been formed by the ancestors or by supernatural forces. Thus the River Lophis originated as the blood of a murdered boy. At the same time, there is the possibility of more basic misunderstandings. Until the development of scientific geology, a series of rock formations were identified by antiquarians as megalithic monuments (Evans 1994). There is no reason why similar errors could not have been made by other people, and there is plenty of place name evidence to suggest that this was in fact what happened.

Natural places have an archaeology because they acquired a significance in the *minds* of people in the past. That did not necessarily make any impact on their outward appearance, but one way of recognising the importance of these locations is through the evidence of human activity that is discovered there. Deposits of artefacts or animal bones, such as those at Ukonsaari, may provide one obvious clue, but there are several more. Pausanias commented on the number of altars on the mountains of Attica, and in other cases the natural surfaces associated with these sites might themselves have been embellished. Not far from the Mesolithic cemetery of Olenii Ostrov there are rock carvings that depict the very artefacts that occur in the graves. There are other connections that seem at least equally plausible: some of the main groups of carved rocks in Scandinavia are located near to the rapids that are so important in Arctic mythology (Tilley 1991a: Chapter 9), and the Minoan frescoes at Thera seem to emphasise the special significance of mountain tops (Morgan 1988: 31–3). The point that has to be emphasised is that what are often described as 'art works' may have been closely connected with the role of natural places.

Relics of those places may even have been removed for use elsewhere. This was obviously the case in Classical Greece, where some of the trees and forests assumed a sacred identity. In one case quoted by Pausanias, a particular oak tree was selected by observing the behaviour of the birds. Then it was shaped into an idol and sacrificed along with slaughtered animals. Perhaps we can make too much of the fact that the idol was burnt on a mountain top, for it is just as important to appreciate the special character of the place where the wood was obtained. A useful comparison is with the sacred building at Newgrange, part of which was made out of materials brought from other parts of Ireland (Mitchell 1992). Rather than describing the ways in which the materials were used in its construction, it might be worth considering the significance of the places from which they were originally acquired. These places may have had monuments of their own, but their chief importance could be in what was taken away from them.

Not all these locations remained unaltered for ever. Some entirely natural places, such as springs, caves or rock formations, attracted later monuments around them. This seems to be what happened at the peak sanctuaries of Bronze Age Crete, where buildings were erected at the same time as the creation of palaces on the lower ground (Rutkowski 1986: Chapter 5). The same sequence may apply to many of the sites visited by Pausanias, where temples, altars and statues were found beside springs or caves. A more subtle variant of this practice is where monuments make explicit reference to features in the wider landscape. They may be aligned on the heavenly bodies, but they can also be orientated towards hills or rock outcrops. Sometimes the relationship is even closer. For example, it seems as if one group of Swedish megaliths was constructed to imitate the appearance of the nearby mountains – a connection that even extended to the choice of materials used to build them (Tilley 1991b) – whilst a group of Neolithic henges in Britain seems to have been laid out to reflect the course followed by nearby rivers (Richards 1996a).

To some extent the discussion has been based on the examples introduced in Chapter 1, but if this account is to be any more than anecdotal, it needs to be pursued at an altogether larger scale. There are certain important questions to be asked. How were natural places used? How significant were these uses in ancient society, and how did they compare with the activities associated with monuments? In what ways can our understanding of natural places in the past modify our interpretation of the landscape as a whole? The implications of these questions extend from abstract theory to the nature of archaeological fieldwork.

Natural practices

In attempting to specify what I mean by an archaeology of natural places, I have already highlighted a series of striking phenomena. They were illustrated by examples that had featured in Chapters 1 and 2, but they might equally have been compared with ethnographic evidence taken from outside Europe. There seemed to be at least three cases in which the significance of such locations could be demonstrated by archaeological evidence. First there were the distinctive deposits that could be associated with natural locations like the Ukonsaari cave or the Minoan peak sanctuaries. Then there were the numerous sites where striking features of the landscape had been embellished by what is loosely described as 'art'. These extended from the rock carvings found near Olenii Ostrov to the altars that Pausanias encountered on the sacred mountains of Attica, and there were also those places whose special significance might be betrayed by the curious way in which they were employed as a source of relics. That point was illustrated by the stones used at Newgrange, but there may be a more general point at issue here. If many of the artefacts deposited at natural locations possessed a special significance through their use in ritual, it may be that the places where they were made, and the processes that took place there, had special connotations too. We have seen this in the selection of material for the idol that was sacrificed at the festival near Plataia, and it may also explain why a large group of unfinished pewter artefacts was deposited by the Saami at the edge of a Swedish lake. Lastly, there is the approach adopted by Tilley (1994) in his studies of the British land-scape, for there are numerous well-documented cases in which locations with a long-established significance were elaborated as monuments at a late stage in their development. The construction of buildings at the Minoan peak sanctuaries is a good example of this process.

All these phenomena have been recognised for some time. The paradox is that they have been investigated quite independently and as research projects that have little connection with the study of the ancient landscape. Their common source in an archaeology of natural places has yet to be acknowledged.

Votive deposits

Again it is worth beginning with votive deposits. Although they play a prominent role in modern archaeology, their study still shows certain limitations. In this case, some attention has been paid to the places in which they are found, but that is intrinsic to the definition of these collections of material: artefacts deposited in springs or rivers are less likely to have been hidden for safe-keeping than those found inside settlements; finds of metalwork stand out when they occur in a mountain pass. They assume a special character in the literature *because of the circumstances in which they were deposited* (Hänsel and Hänsel 1997).

Once more, the places where this happened attract less discussion than the processes that account for these deposits. In the case of portable artefacts, especially those from distant sources, these finds represent the end of a life cycle: the point at which the history of production and exchange finally came to an end. Indeed, the deposition of these items may have had implications for the system as a whole by reducing the supply of similar material in circulation (Kristiansen 1978); more probably, it protected its special character by preventing its use in an unsuitable manner (Meillassoux 1968). Artefacts that were intended for deployment in particular kinds of transaction had to be withdrawn from circulation when those transactions were complete. The most obvious example is where specialised artefacts could not be inherited but had to be destroyed on the death of their owner.

Like other rituals, such transactions could be manipulated and might change from one generation to another. This process has also been studied in detail, as one of the ways in which groups or individuals competed for political power. Perhaps they did so by making increasingly lavish gifts to the gods. This was both a source of prestige and a way of taking valuables out of circulation so that they could not fall into the hands of rivals (Gregory 1980). It seems possible that extravagant consumption of this kind replaced the more parsimonious offerings of grave goods during the course of the Bronze Age, and yet this practice was attended by some fairly strict conventions. These concerned the relationship between the kinds of material being consumed and the kinds of places in which such deposits were appropriate (Hansen 1991). Thus tools are often found on dry land, and weapons in rivers and lakes. It seems as if the careers of certain types of artefact were ordained from the time of their production. There were places in which they could be deposited and places where that would not have been right, but always the emphasis has been on the objects themselves. We might turn the question round and ask how particular kinds of places could have been used over time. What kinds of offerings had to be provided there? And which were unacceptable?

Too much emphasis was placed on the practical aspects of technology, so that these obvious distinctions were blurred. Many writers, myself included, have attempted to distinguish between votive and utilitarian hoards, defining the latter group as those connected with the production and distribution of metalwork. Thus some of these collections have been interpreted as groups of finished items stored together before their distribution by the smith, whilst others seemed to be made up of scrap metal collected for recycling. The common feature is that these are usually found in dry land and could have been recovered, although there is no indication as to why the smith should so often have failed to do so. The interpretation of these deposits as everyday or 'utilitarian' is convincing only if we consider the transformation of the metal as a straightforward process; but the more that we learn about where it was carried out and how the finished products were consumed, the less likely this seems to be (Budd and Taylor 1995). The places where these collections occur deserve a more searching analysis.

Lastly, what applies to deposits of artefacts also applies to other kinds of material. Deposits of bones are too often taken for granted and treated as domestic waste, but one important development of recent years has been the attempt to investigate their composition and even their configuration in the ground (Thomas 1991: Chapter 4). That is especially important when they are found in apparent isolation, or in combination with distinctive or unusual objects. Archaeologists have, however, paid more attention to the contents of these collections than they have to the character of the places where they are found. Either the bones are treated, quite misleadingly, as evidence of the subsistence economy, or they are interpreted as the surviving residue of important transactions such as feasts. In neither case is it asked why they should be found at distinctive places in the landscape, and that is where a new study might begin.

Rock art

The link between rock art and the natural topography is seemingly much more straightforward. Except in those rare cases where fragments of already decorated stone were moved, the painted or carved motifs are fixed at a particular point in the landscape. Yet it is not a feature that has played an important part in studies of this evidence. Either rock art has been considered on an essentially local scale, such as the relationship of Palaeolithic images to the micro-topography of French caves (Clottes 1996), or it has been treated at a more general level, as we can see from those studies that relate the rock carvings of Scandinavia to the changing coastline (Bertilsson 1987). In the latter case, this can shed important light on their relationship to wider tracts of the prehistoric landscape – settlement areas, for instance, or the areas with burial cairns – but such careful attention to the topography still remains rather unusual. The main concern is with images.

It seems somewhat perverse that the individual motifs in European rock art are so often treated by prehistorians in the same manner as portable artefacts. They are classified and compared, their associations are noted and used to form a chronology, and the wider distributions of these different elements are grouped together to define styles and regional groups (Malmer 1981). There is more interest in the artefact types depicted in these paintings and drawings than there is in the contexts in which they were created, and the web of associations and superimpositions worked out at sites like Valcamonica assume almost the same form as the records of a major excavation (Anati 1994).

Rock art is often analysed following similar preconceptions to studies of portable objects, and for that reason the results of this work can become inconclusive or overextended. Exactly the same point can be made about the study of prehistoric metalwork. In fact, that comparison can be taken even further. Until relatively recently, the analysis of metal artefacts showed little awareness of the true potential of its subject matter. The available material was organised according to its associations in the closed groups known as hoards, but too many scholars were uninterested in the reasons why these collections were formed or the places where that happened. The images found in rock art are rather like those deposits: they contain a particular group of signs brought together in a particular place. It is profitable to think of metalwork deposits in terms of the relationship between a prescribed selection of artefacts and an appropriate point in the landscape. The contents of prehistoric rock art describe a similar kind of relationship, and the two act together to establish the significance of that location (Whitley 1998).

Beyond the interest in organising and classifying rock art, there has always been a concern with its meaning, but many studies of this kind overlook one vital element. Unlike speech, song or even dance, rock art provides a method of communication that can be decidedly unilateral. That is to say, both parties to that interchange need not be present on the same occasion. The painted or carved surfaces can speak for them in their absence – provided the message is comprehensible. The vital element to consider is the intended audience: both the numbers of people to whom these images are addressed and the occasions on which they will encounter them (Gamble 1991). If we are to examine that question at all, we must be able to say more about the character of the places that were chosen for this purpose. The 'art' cannot be treated as if it were sufficient in itself.

In short, rock art can be characterised as the marking of places by signs, but it is the signs that have dominated the discussion so far. They are undoubtedly important, but if they formed part of a wider system of communication – sacred or profane – it is reasonable to suppose that different surfaces might be marked in different ways (if that did not happen, then the high degree of redundancy would be worth investigating in its own right). The appropriate scale for studying this question is the landscape as a whole, for it is the wider network of places that will ultimately define its special character. In many cases that broader network will also draw in the monuments that have attracted so much attention already.

Production sites

The study of production sites raises problems of a different kind, for these have been investigated and understood in terms of ancient technologies. That is to say, they are primarily a source of information about how people extracted raw materials from their environment in order to live their lives more efficiently (Torrence 1986). That model formed the basis of the Three Age System developed in the nineteenth century, and, although this scheme has long been criticised, some of the attitudes that lay behind it still influence archaeology today. Thus mining or quarrying were obviously undertaken to provide the most suitable material for blade tools, despite the fact that perfectly adequate stone could sometimes be obtained from surface exposures. In the same way, the working of copper and bronze was believed to replace earlier technologies because these materials provided more effective tools. The same reasoning applied to the introduction of iron. Prehistorians have long accepted that the situation was more complicated than that. Copper and bronze may have been adopted because of their exotic qualities and were often used to make objects that were essentially items of display (Renfrew 1986). In the same way, iron does not seem to have been an acceptable substitute for bronze in the votive deposits of later prehistoric Europe, and it was long after the inception of what is commonly characterised as the 'Iron Age' that this inhibition broke down (Bradley 1990a: 150–4).

Such points are increasingly widely accepted, but their implications have not been followed to their logical conclusion. There is still a tendency to stress the practical side of artefact production, even when the deposition of those same objects took place in a ritual context. Unless archaeologists are able to show how 'mundane' objects could aspire to a more specialised role, it may be unwise to make any assumptions about the places where they were produced. Ethnographic studies of such different activities as stone axe production in New Guinea (Burton 1984) and iron working in Africa (Barndon 1996) must surely alert us to the complexity of the processes involved. That is what has been lacking in European archaeology. If the use of particular materials, such as stones or metals, extended outside our normal understanding of technology, the sites where those materials were obtained call for a more careful analysis.

Not all these studies have been restricted to questions of technology, but where they have followed a more ambitious course they have been concerned largely with exchange. This is an important step and one that is both logical and necessary. It is logical because so much effort has already been invested in the characterisation of artefacts. It began as a largely descriptive exercise, resulting in increasingly plausible attempts to link the findspots of individual objects to the places where they were made. The problem was to study the missing term of that equation: to analyse the mechanisms by which they were distributed. At the same time, the rapprochement between archaeology and anthropology in Europe resulted in a growing awareness of the strategic role played by exchange in non-market societies. Here was an opportunity to study how production, circulation and consumption were related to one another in the lives of prehistoric people (Bradley and Edmonds 1993). Indeed, archaeologists increasingly favoured a 'biographical' approach to the artefacts themselves (Kopytoff 1986).

There are numerous problems concerning the sources from which prehistoric artefacts derive. As we shall see, stone axe quarries might be located on inaccessible islands when similar stone could have been obtained on the mainland. They could be sited on remote and even dangerous mountain peaks, even though equally suitable raw material could be acquired more easily on the lower ground. Bronze artefacts may have been made at the sites of burial mounds, and prehistoric iron working sometimes took place inside the sacred monuments of an earlier period. Once we accept that these places were possibly as important as the things that were made there, it becomes easier to understand how materials that had no 'practical' function whatever might also be transported across country. The bluestones incorporated in Stonehenge provide one obvious example (Green 1997; Scourse 1997). Production sites may have been studied as evidence of technology and exchange, but these were probably places that possessed a special significance in their own right, and that has still to be investigated.

Monumental architecture

I have left monuments until the end of this section, although that is not because they were unimportant. No doubt they were vitally linked with the system of natural places described up to now. Many of them will have originated in long established ways of using special locations, and even when their outer form changed they may have maintained their close relationship with places that did not develop in the same way. The important point is to recognise that monuments cannot be considered in isolation. They will be easier to interpret when that background is properly researched. They have often been studied in rather abstract terms, as exercises in prehistoric ergonomics, as status symbols or as 'central places' (Moore 1996; Renfrew 1973). None of these approaches is sufficiently integrated into the archaeology of the local landscape. If that avenue of research is to prosper, it will be necessary to work on a very different scale. Above all, we need to investigate the archaeology of monuments alongside that of 'natural' places.

To some extent this has already been attempted, and in certain respects research is much further advanced than it is in the other fields considered in this chapter. In his book *A Phenomenology of Landscape*, Christopher Tilley attempts to recreate the perceptions of individuals in the past (Tilley 1994). This method has been applied most successfully to the use of specific monuments, where the human actors are framed by architectural features that guide their movements and control the sequence in which different spaces can be experienced. It has led to important insights into the use of megalithic tombs and the ways in which famous structures like Avebury and Stonehenge might have been perceived. It has been more difficult to apply to the landscape as a whole, and in fact the principal studies have taken monuments of one kind or another as their point of departure. Thus they seek to describe the experience of moving along specific paths, like the Dorset Cursus or the avenues at Avebury or Stonehenge (Barrett 1994: Chapters 1 and 2; Tilley 1994: Chapter 5). They consider the siting and orientation of megalithic tombs in relation to the natural backdrop provided by rocks and hills (Tilley 1994: Chapters 3 and 4), or interpret the Neolithic enclosures in south-west England in relation to the extraordinary granite outcrops known as tors (Tilley 1996).

That is both the strength and the weakness of this approach. At its best it certainly enlarges our understanding of individual monuments and results in quite specific observations whose importance might otherwise have gone unnoticed. I can testify to the value of this approach at those sites that I know well myself, in particular the Dorset Cursus where I worked some years ago (Barrett *et al.* 1991: 35–68). The problem is that it is almost impossible to assess the insights provided by these studies without repeating them on the ground, for they have not been conducted with an explicit methodology in mind. As a result, there is no simple way of deciding whether the authors' observations are significant or whether the patterns that they describe could have come about by chance. Since much of this writing is concerned with the individual experience of encountering and interpreting these sites, such criticism may seem misplaced, and no doubt it would be rejected by the original authors. Their work is explicitly concerned with their subjective responses to the landscape, and in those terms it has its own validity. I would like to be able to use their interpretations in my own research, but I am not sure whether I can do so, since my response to the same places may not be the same as theirs. Ideally, I would like to assess their readings of the landscape by comparing the attributes of the places that they studied with those of a series of 'control samples' where similar phenomena should not occur. This amounts to allying the methodology of processual archaeology to the agenda of post-processualism. This is very much the premise of research based on the use of Geographical Information Systems (Lock and Stancic 1995), but it can also be followed on the ground. I have tried to put this into practice in some studies of British rock art (Bradley 1997: Chapter 5).

There is a second, more serious problem with the approach illustrated by Tilley in *A Phenomenology of Landscape* (Tilley 1994). As I said earlier, this work is very much concerned with the wider setting of monuments. Although he is aware of landscapes in which similar constructions are lacking, such features as rocks, mountains and rivers enter his interpretation only because of their relationship to these buildings. In one case, megalithic tombs use impressive rocks to provide a monumental backdrop; in another, they are aligned on a prominent mountain. Tilley accounts for the placing of these particular tombs through a kind of retro-spection: such structures must have been built there because those natural features were already important in the experience of local hunter gatherers. In this way, he believes, he can also point to elements in Mesolithic sacred geography. He takes this approach to the tor enclosures on Bodmin Moor, where there seems little doubt that Neolithic people did embellish a series of natural rock outcrops (Tilley 1996). Again he suggests that this happened because these strange landforms must have assumed a special importance in the lives of local hunter gatherers, but without such a clear relationship between the walled enclosures and the tors, it would have been difficult to advance the same interpretation.

And that is the problem. Is it possible to discuss the role of entirely unaltered features of the natural landscape? Can such places be studied to any purpose in areas where monuments are absent? The ethnographic evidence from many parts of the world may suggest that such features as caves and mountains had a special significance, but is there any way of assessing whether this was actually the case? I suggest that this is perfectly feasible, provided the analysis stays close to those areas where there is archaeological material available for study.

Retrospect

I have commented on the research that has been carried out in four different fields. In each case it has been undertaken with a specific agenda in mind. The results have been important and influential, but at the same time they have been too limited, so that few connections have been made between these different subjects. It is the right time to try again.

I have been working on this subject for nearly fifteen years, but it was only recently that I realised this. This illustrates my contention that in preparing thematic studies of particular bodies of material, archaeologists can easily lose sight of the deeper connections between them. Each of the topics considered in the previous section of this chapter has formed the subject of an earlier project of my own. Having described two journeys in the previous chapters – those of Arthur Evans and Pausanias – I would like to conclude Part 1 of this book by retracing my own journey through that material.

This almost unconscious programme of research began with a series of studies of prehistoric metal hoards. These were largely concerned with discussing how the deposition of wealth may have been used in prehistoric societies in northern and western Europe: an enquiry that I thought of at the time as a contribution to 'social archaeology' (Bradley 1990b). Although those studies of metalwork eventually extended into an account of other kinds of votive deposit, the main role of natural places in my work was as 'receptacles' for this kind of material. Despite the use made of distribution maps, their wider significance as places was not a major issue. Instead I emphasised the more abstract properties of *space*.

Over the same period, and in collaboration with Mark Edmonds, I attempted to look at the other extreme in the life history of specialised artefacts. For three years we mounted a field investigation of the Neolithic axe quarries at Great Langdale in Cumbria, seeking to relate the changing methods used in production there to more general tendencies in the distribution and consumption of those artefacts. To some extent we did acknowledge the extraordinary character of this place and the many ways in which its use departed from purely practical considerations (Bradley and Edmonds 1993). A different kind of study might have taken this observation as its starting point, but in fact it was a possibility that developed during the course of our fieldwork.

To some extent, the experience of working on that site did influence my perspective on landscape archaeology and, in particular, on the role of natural places. I sought to develop this perspective through a study of the rock art of Britain and Ireland, extending the investigation to Continental Europe in collaboration with Felipe Criado and Ramón Fábregas. This certainly emphasised the role played by petroglyphs at a number of different levels, from defining access to resources and delimiting areas of settled land to marking sacred places and the routes leading between them. But this project still had a traditional aspect, for it was also concerned with investigating cultural relations between different communities along the Atlantic coastline (Bradley 1997). On that level, I still retained my interest in the analysis of style. Only in a more recent project, again conducted jointly with Dr Fábregas, has the full importance of natural places in the Iberian landscape become clear to me (Bradley and Fábregas 1998). Some of that fieldwork is described in Chapter 5.

Lastly, when I was beginning my research on Atlantic rock art, I was invited to give the Rhind Lectures in Edinburgh and chose to talk about 'The Origins of Monuments' (Bradley 1993). This was a wonderful opportunity to try out some new ideas, but they were necessarily presented in a much abbreviated form. Each lecture could have been a book in itself, but, mercifully, this was not permitted. The first of these lectures considered the relationship between domestication and the onset of monument building, and the second discussed the ways in which such structures may have developed out of places with an already established significance. It was frustrating that there was so much left to say. That first lecture eventually expanded into another publication, *The Significance of Monuments* (Bradley 1998a). Now it is the turn of the second one. After fifteen years of tackling this topic obliquely, I prefer to approach it head on. That is what I shall try to do in the remaining sections of this book.

Part 2

Explorations

There is a voice, not understood by all,
Sent from these desert-caves.

Shelley, cancelled passage from 'Mont Blanc', Garnett 1862

Chapter 4

Presenting arms

The locations of votive deposits in prehistoric Europe

This chapter suggests an approach to the archaeology of hoards and votive deposits influenced by the studies in Part I. Rather than investigating the contents of these collections through the history of different kinds of artefact, it considers the significance of specific places in the landscape and the ways in which they were treated. The evidence extends from the selection of those localities for particular kinds of offering to the composition of the groups of people who may have used them. Changes over time are important too. The argument is illustrated by the Neolithic bog finds of Denmark and by Bronze Age metalwork from northern and western Europe.

Introduction

In Part 1 I sketched some of the characteristics of an archaeology of natural places, using two very different examples drawn from European ethnography. Each of them described an area in which such accounts could be related directly to archaeological evidence.

What is the usefulness of such an exercise? There is an obvious temptation to take these examples literally, especially when they have so many features in common. Can they 'stand for' past practices that are beyond the reach of archaeology, or should they be treated simply as a source of inspiration? In fact, both approaches may have something to offer. Each example can be useful as a source of ideas in itself, to be investigated entirely in terms of archaeological evidence, but there is also the possibility that some of the specific practices recorded among the Saami echo the beliefs of their own ancestors during the prehistoric period.

Chapter 1 began with Arthur Evans's excavation in the cave of Ukonsaari and developed into a more general account of votive or sacrificial sites in the archaeology of northern Scandinavia. Part 2 of this book has a similar point of departure, but is mainly concerned with the prehistory of other parts of Europe where the question of direct connections is unlikely to apply. Nevertheless, the detail in which Saami sacrificial sites have been documented does introduce a range of unfamiliar questions.

One of the most rewarding ways of considering the hoards of prehistoric

Europe has been to consider the 'biographies' of the objects that were deposited there. To quote Kopytoff:

> Where does the thing come from and who made it? What has been its career so far and what do people consider to be an ideal career for such things? What are the recognised 'ages' or periods in the thing's 'life', and what are the cultural markers for them? How does the thing's use change with its age, *and what happens to it when it reaches the end of its usefulness?*
>
> (Kopytoff 1986: 66–7; my emphasis)

For example, it is possible to consider the contexts in which Bronze Age weapons were made, principally through an investigation of their metal composition or the remains of moulds (Mordant *et al.* 1998). The history of these weapons might be recovered through a detailed examination of the artefacts themselves: had they been used in combat, had they been repaired or resharpened and did they show any signs of wear? The contexts of the surviving objects could also be investigated. Many of these artefacts had been deposited in rivers or other watery locations: had they been damaged when this happened, or were any of them in pristine condition (Bridgford 1997)? Were they associated with other kinds of archaeological material – not only artefacts but human and animal bones (Healy and Housley 1992)? Some weapons might have been broken up so that the metal could be reused, and in certain circumstances the smith may have deposited part of this material in dry land.

An alternative approach is suggested by the accounts considered in Chapters 1 and 2. Instead of considering the cultural biography of the objects that were used as offerings, we could turn our attention to the biographies of the different *places* where that process happened. The ethnography of the Saami suggests a number of questions that have still to be answered by prehistorians working in northern and western Europe; to a lesser extent, the same is true of the writings of Pausanias. For example, specific kinds of places may have been used for specific offerings, and these may have been associated with different groups of people. These places were dedicated to particular supernatural powers, and the sacrifices that took place there may have been made with a variety of purposes in mind.

I can illustrate each of these propositions using the sources cited so far. Among the Saami, for instance, there is a fundamental distinction between the *siejddes* associated with sacrifices of reindeer and those used for sacrificing fish. To a large extent this is because these locations occupy distinctive settings in the landscape. The people who visited them would have been engaged in different kinds of food production, and the same offerings would not have been appropriate in every case (Manker 1957). Different gods might also demand different kinds of sacrifice. For instance, white reindeer were offered to the sun god and uncastrated animals to the god of thunder, whilst black animals were associated with the forces of death. In some cases the sacred drum told the Saami that their sacrifices must contain unusual elements, such as domesticated animals which had to be introduced for the purpose (Rydving 1995).

That close relationship between particular places and particular kinds of offering is also evidenced by the dedication of the sacrificial sites. Among the Saami, mountains might be associated with individual gods, whilst the ancestral spirits of women were linked with certain lakes (Manker 1957). We find a similar set of contrasts in the Classical world. The gods had their own attributes and this meant that it was appropriate to worship them in quite specific places. To give just two examples, the sea god, Poseidon, was associated with underground waters and the seashore, whilst the special position of Zeus in the Greek pantheon was celebrated by the creation of sanctuaries on mountain tops (Burkert 1985: 125 and 136). These divinities had their own sphere of influence, and it follows that offerings might be provided for a whole variety of reasons, and at different places in the landscape.

Lastly, the offerings made by the Saami were of two basic forms, both of which seem to have their counterparts in prehistoric Europe. There were the sites that were associated with idols and with large numbers of animal bones (Manker 1957). There were also examples that contained metal artefacts (Figure 11). The latter date from a limited period in which native people in the Arctic seem to have been drawn into the fur trade. This resulted in an unprecedented influx of wealth, and imported metalwork was deposited at the sacrificial sites over a period of 350 years (Mulk 1996).

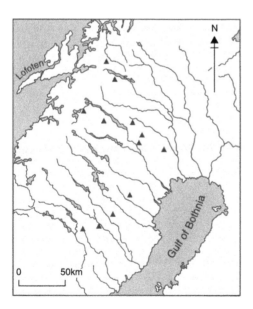

Figure 11 The distribution of Saami metal finds
Source: Data from Zachrisson 1984

The main items came from Scandinavia, Germany, Finland, Russia and the eastern Baltic. They included a variety of ornaments as well as coins, which were often perforated for suspension (Figure 12). A number of pewter artefacts were locally made. The metalwork from the sacrificial sites was probably used mainly as amulets or pendants, and there is evidence that some of them had been attached to idols or to reindeer antlers. Others may have been fixed to the shamans' drums. It seems likely that certain metals were thought to have special powers (Zachrisson 1984).

The deposition of metalwork was only an episode in a longer history of sacrificial offerings, and it was confined to the period when the Saami were engaged in long-distance exchange. There have been several explanations of why imported objects were offered to the gods. Mulk (1996) compares these metal finds to the north-west American institution of the potlatch, and suggests that they were undertaken to avoid the threat to the social order caused by an influx of private wealth. In her terms, the offerings of metalwork represent a levelling mechanism, used to maintain an egalitarian society. Storli, on the other hand, believes that they represent accumulations of valuables offered to the supernatural in accordance with the Norse 'Law of Odin' (Storli 1996). By depositing treasure in this way, people secured their riches in the afterlife. Whatever the answer, it is clear that the Saami metal finds are altogether exceptional.

Somewhat paradoxically, these patterns are the exact opposite of those in prehistoric Europe, where the deposits containing Bronze Age metalwork have been treated as the norm. Like the material just described, they include imported artefacts or objects made from foreign raw materials. These have been documented in much more detail than their simpler equivalents: so much so that in some regions only part of the phenomenon has been studied. As a result, most of the questions asked in this chapter must be investigated using the evidence of metal finds, for these allow the basic issues to be discussed. Only when that has been done can we turn our attention to the deposits of food remains and other

Figure 12 Examples of Saami metal finds
Source: Based on information in Zachrisson 1984

artefacts. As we shall see, these have more in common with the Saami votive deposits.

How far can the same themes be studied in the archaeology of northern and western Europe? The first question is perhaps the easiest to address.

Offering places

In Bronze Age Europe the character of the different deposits seems to have been influenced by the places in which they were made. There is no doubt that in many regions particular kinds of locations were treated in special ways. The problem is that these conventions arose as a result of local traditions and were not uniform over large areas. They also changed over time.

In the Later Bronze Age, there is one excavated site that illustrates a number of these issues. On the Fen edge in eastern England is the remarkable site of Flag Fen. Although this is not yet published in final form, its most important character-istics are already apparent from an interim report (Pryor 1992). Flag Fen itself was a substantial wooden platform attached to a timber roadway leading across shal-low water between two densely occupied areas of dry land. Although the platform was associated with a number of structured deposits, including pottery, metalwork and animal remains, it was the post alignment that was associated with the widest variety of finds. At its eastern limit, it meets the water's edge close to the Bronze Age field ditches at Fengate; indeed, its alignment follows the same axis as those land divisions.

The site was in use over a long period. The wooden posts date from between about 1350 and 950 BC, whilst the metalwork suggests that artefacts were being deposited here over 1,200 years. This practice came to an end only during the Iron Age. There were important changes in how the area was used, and it seems as if offerings of weapons were especially important in the earlier part of the sequence, whilst ornaments such as brooches and pins played a more prominent role in later years. The natural environment also changed over that period as the fen basin was invaded by water.

This site is so important because the deposits have been investigated in the field. In most cases, the finds from wet locations are chance discoveries, recovered by peat digging or dredging, with the result that little is known about their original contexts. Moreover, it is likely that certain kinds of material, including bones and the smaller pieces of metalwork, were often overlooked. In the Flag Fen complex, there are three types of location and four different kinds of deposit. The most basic distinction is between the material found on the fen edge, where the land may have been dry for part of the year, and the remaining finds which were probably placed in shallow water (Figure 13). At the same time, it seems as if different kinds of material were deposited on either side of the alignment of posts.

Towards the end of the alignment, where it meets dry land, the distributions of three categories overlap: tools, ornaments and weapons. To some extent, these are kept separate in the areas that would have been wet all year round. Although there

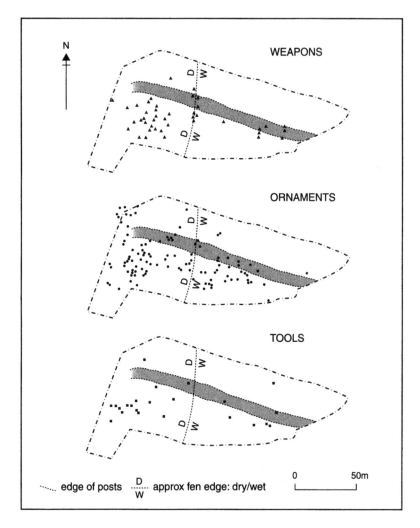

Figure 13 Plan of the excavated area at Flag Fen, eastern England
Source: Data from Pryor 1992

are no sharp boundaries, the finds of weaponry are most abundant towards the land, where an area of pasture was threatened by the rising water, whilst the ornaments extended further out and must have been deposited in places that were permanently wet. Tools were deposited over a wider area and are found in the same parts of the site as both ornaments and weapons. On the other hand, almost all the metalwork was to the south of the timber causeway. To its north, excavation revealed a completely different kind of deposit consisting mainly of animal bones. These had an unusual composition, for whilst they did include the remains of food, they also contained the skeletons of dogs. It is possible that other animals entered the water as complete carcasses. The same part of the site contained a number of disarticulated human bones.

Thus at least three different kinds of material were separated from one another at Flag Fen. Many of the weapons were offered towards the limits of dry land, whilst some of the ornaments were deposited in deeper water. The finds of metalwork occupied a different part of the site from the animal and human bones. Each collection has unusual characteristics. Animal burials are known on living sites of the Later Bronze Age, but the emphasis on dogs is exceptional. Much of the metalwork had been damaged before it was deposited on the site, and a number of artefacts were so poorly made that they may have been intended as votives from the outset; there is even a little evidence that they had been made nearby. Others were entirely exotic and include unusual forms that must have been imported from the Continent. Even the finds of implements have a distinctive character. Although their distribution overlaps with those of the other artefacts, they include an exceptional range of metalworking tools.

It would be wrong to suggest that Flag Fen provides an appropriate analogy for the full range of votive deposits in Britain – still less those in northern and western Europe – but it does illustrate one vital point that it shares with Saami archaeology: *different kinds of deposit might be made in different places*. There is no reason to expect the same specific relationships to be found in other areas. The basic principle is more significant than the details.

Similar distinctions are found very widely. The most basic was undoubtedly that between wet deposits and those on dry land, and in other areas this is often associated with deposits of weapons and tools respectively. Finds of ornaments show a less consistent pattern, and in different regions they tend to occur in either of these contexts. The important point is that in any particular area they exhibit a clear preference for only one of these locations. Tools, weapons and ornaments are also found together in what are often interpreted as collections of 'scrap metal'. These were usually buried on dry land. It seems as if different kinds of location were used to deposit different kinds of material, and there is little overlap between the contents of these collections (Bradley 1990a: Chapter 3).

Excavation at Flag Fen allows us to recognise small-scale distinctions in the distributions of particular deposits. These subtleties have sometimes been apparent on a regional scale. The finds from wet locations often exhibit a considerable diversity. In Ireland, for example, different kinds of material were placed in rivers, bogs, springs and lakes (Needham 1988). The distribution of particular types of artefacts might change from one location to another over time, and all the river finds cannot be treated in the same ways. In the north of Hesse, weapons are associated with the major rivers, but pins were deposited in shallow water (Kubach 1983). Here the main distinction seems to have been one of access. The weapons may have been dropped from boats, whilst small ornaments could have entered the water from the riverbank. Even within the major rivers, certain places seem to have been specially favoured for making offerings, and the finds of archaeological material are not uniformly distributed. Detailed studies even show that different stretches of these rivers may have been associated with different kinds of deposit. Although the Thames contains one of the highest densities of Later Bronze Age weaponry in Europe, the main groups of material are found in separate lengths of the river from one period to the next (Needham and Burgess 1980). Moreover, recent work at Eton has recovered a distinctive series of deposits from which metalwork is entirely absent. Instead, there were groups of human and animal bones, principally skulls. Some of these were accompanied by ceramics, and their positions were marked by posts (Tim Allen pers. comm.). It seems likely that certain stretches of the river were treated in quite specific ways.

Dry land finds may be equally diverse. For example, there are deposits associated with caves and rock fissures and groups of metalwork and other artefacts from hill tops or mountain passes (Bianco Peroni 1979). The positions of some of these deposits seem to have been marked, perhaps by stones or by distinctive outcrops, but this was not always the case. Others were inserted into the remains of older monuments, from occupation sites to megalithic tombs. Sometimes these places can be fitted into a broader scheme. For example, among the most distinctive deposits are those from caves containing underground rivers. Here there is perhaps a link with the water finds. Indeed, the metalwork recovered from rock fissures includes deposits of half-melted raw material, very similar to those encountered in dry land hoards where they have been viewed as the remains of a workshop. The fact that this material was virtually inaccessible after its deposition suggests that another interpretation might be more appropriate (Maier 1977; Schauer 1981).

A 'biographical' approach would emphasise the changing history of these places. There was considerable variation over time. In the Danish Bronze Age, for example, the percentage of ornament hoards from bogs fluctuated between about 50 per cent and 70 per cent of the locations that have adequate records, and the finds of scrap metal were mainly in dry land locations in Periods II and IV, when these account for between 75 per cent and 82 per cent of the finds (the sample from Period III is too small to be significant). They changed to bogs and similar places in Period V, when 65 per cent of these collections were associated with water. Deposits of weapons and tools become less common over the same period, but again they show a striking association with a particular kind of site. Virtually all the weapons are associated with wet places and nearly all the tool hoards were on dry land (Levy 1982).

Table 1 sets out the preferred locations for each of these groups and the few details that are known about the character of individual findspots. These examples come from Periods II, IV, V and VI – those with the largest groups of material. Again it is clear that certain types of location were appropriate for particular kinds of deposit.

Table 1 The changing locations of metal deposits in Bronze Age Denmark

Main location	Other detailed locations	Contents
Period II:		
Wet	Bog, cliff, natural mound	Ornaments
Wet	Bog, spring, stream	Weapons
Dry	Under large stones	Tools
Period IV:		
Wet and dry	Bog, cliff, hill, barrow, natural mound	Ornaments
Dry	Mound, megalith, hill, under large stones	Scrap metal
Period V:		
Wet	Bog, well, cliff, hill, megalith, under large stones	Ornaments
Wet	Bog, stream	Weapons
Wet	Bog, megalith, under stone	Scrap metal
Period VI:		
Wet	Bog, hill, under stone, fjord	Ornaments

Source: Levy 1982

Identifying the participants

In the ethnographic cases considered earlier it is clear that particular locations and practices were limited to particular groups of people, on the basis of age and gender. Women, for example, were not allowed to visit the Saami sacrificial sites. Indeed, their presence was one way in which the Christian missionaries attempted to desecrate these places (Rydving 1995: 66). In other societies, the situation might be very different. One example from Classical antiquity was the cult of Dionysus, who was worshipped by women at his mountain sanctuaries (Buxton 1994: 94–5). Such sacred places were not only dedicated to separate deities, but the offerings that were made there came from different sections of the population.

Is it possible to identify similar principles at work in prehistoric Europe? It is all too tempting to reproduce modern prejudices about the significance of different artefacts and their links with different categories of people, so that weapons have exclusively male associations and ornaments are associated with women. The same applies to the high status assigned to fine objects, although the fact that so many of them use large quantities of non-local raw materials may lend some support to this idea. The best procedure is to rely as far as possible on their *archaeological* associations.

These would certainly suggest that 'wet finds' enjoyed a special status. The evidence from Britain and Ireland provides two arguments in favour of this idea. The main groups of Later Bronze Age weapons in the rivers are the direct successors of the types in the most complex burials of the Early Bronze Age. At the same time, those associated with ordinary settlements are less elaborate. Taken together, such arguments suggest that some material enjoyed a special status (Bradley 1990a: 99–109). The same is surely true of the gold ornaments found in Irish bogs, for recent work has shown that these deposits were located near to a series of massive hill forts dating from the same period. Such sites seem to have been at the top of the settlement hierarchy. Perhaps the places where those offerings were made were associated with people who enjoyed a special position in society (Grogan *et al.* 1996). It is impossible to tell whether others were allowed to attend these ceremonies.

There is also a case to be made for particular places being associated with either men or women. Rivers are certainly associated with weapons, and similar artefacts are generally found in male graves in other regions. At the same time, some of the metalwork found in the Thames was apparently associated with human skulls of the same period. These do not represent a cross section of the prehistoric population, for the majority (60 per cent) belong to men. Moreover, they are largely limited to young adults. There are very few skulls of adolescents or children, and old people are hardly represented at all. It is not possible to show that the human remains come from the part of the population who deposited this material, but one plausible explanation is that this was a kind of 'river burial' that came into fashion as the single grave tradition lapsed towards the end of the Early Bronze Age (Bradley and Gordon 1988).

In Scandinavian archaeology many of the ornament hoards have been associated with women because similar artefacts occur in female graves in areas further to the south (Figure 14; Gibbs 1987; Levy 1982: Chapter 6; Wels-Weyrauch 1978 and 1991). Like the weapon deposits considered earlier, some of these finds are associated with wet locations. These ornament deposits have one particularly striking characteristic, for they appear in sets. There is a little evidence to suggest that they may have been acquired during the course of a lifetime, because otherwise comparable artefacts can show different amounts of use wear (Taylor 1993: 47–8). If that is correct, it may mean that the sets of ornaments were associated with women of different ages. The fact that many Danish hoards include more than one set (the greatest number is five) could also indicate that they were connected with different numbers of people. Again it is impossible to tell whether these artefacts were deposited by the owners themselves, and it is just as likely that some or all of them were offered when those people had died. The same interpretation may apply to ornament hoards found in other parts of Europe, but it would be wrong to regard them as female equipment unless there are compelling reasons for doing so. It may be enough to suggest that different groups of material were associated with different kinds of people. These distinctions may have extended from the forms of offering that

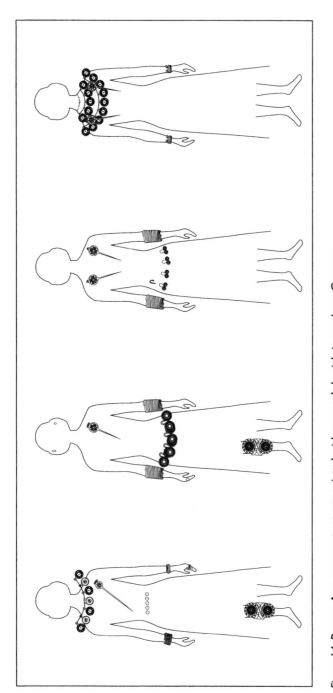

Figure 14 Bronze Age ornament sets associated with women's burials in southern Germany
Source: Information from Wels-Weyrauch 1978

it was appropriate to make to the individuals or groups who were entitled to provide them.

Distinctions of occupation may have been important too. A notable feature of some of the dry land deposits is that their contents seem to be associated with metalworking. This evidence takes many forms, but, as we have seen, these hoards often include a mixture of different artefact types that seem to have been broken up for use as scrap metal. Some of these collections contain casting waste, slag, ingots or even moulds, making the association with smiths especially plausible. The same applies in those cases where freshly cast artefacts were deposited together before they were ready for use. It has been all too easy to propose a practical interpretation of these collections, based on the notion that bronze production was a purely 'economic' activity (Kristiansen 1998: 79–85). The large collections of metalwork of this type are explained as the smith's stock in trade concealed in times of crisis.

This interpretation of some hoards as 'non-ritual' or 'utilitarian' (Levy 1982: Chapter 3) seems increasingly improbable because it fails to provide a satisfactory explanation as to why so much of this material remained in the ground. It seems logical to connect the accumulation of scrap with the recycling of raw material by the smiths, but metal analysis shows that this had been happening for a long time before these hoards made their appearance (Mordant *et al.* 1998). A second objection is much more serious. This entire approach suggests that the smiths themselves operated according to the kind of free enterprise suggested in the late work of Gordon Childe (1958). It is hard to see why supposedly mundane objects should have taken on special connotations *after* they had been produced, and that makes it difficult to explain why so many of them were to end up in unusual contexts like rivers. It may be much more relevant to consider whether the smiths themselves occupied a special position in society. Metalworking is a process that involves particular skills and particular kinds of knowledge. Its procedures are dangerous and arcane, and there is considerable ethnographic evidence to suggest that it might have been accompanied by rituals (Barndon 1996; Herbert 1984; Reid and MacLean 1995). Indeed, that might be why some of the best evidence for metal production comes from places that were well outside the sphere of domestic life. The metal itself could have been imbued with special properties, and it seems possible that the smiths offered some of this highly charged material to the supernatural. One variant of this practice is evidenced in western Germany, where ingots were buried in the graves of a limited section of society (Hansen 1991). In the light of these arguments, it seems as if this distinctive group of deposits was actually made by the smiths responsible for producing the objects.

A further category of deposits is still more difficult to define, but they may have been the work of ritual specialists (Levy 1982: Chapter 8). These are characterised by a limited range of very elaborate objects that lack any obvious function in everyday life. The most convincing examples are figurines, miniature vehicles, such as the Trundholm sun chariot, or the groups of musical instruments that can be found together in bogs. They are mainly a feature of the Scandinavian Bronze

Age, but deposits of similar type are also found in south-west Ireland where the same interpretation may be justified (Eogan 1983: 11–12).

Again, the metal hoards of Bronze Age Denmark show most of these principles at work (Levy 1982). The majority can be divided into two main groups: deposits consisting exclusively of ornaments, weapons or tools, and those that seem to be connected with the transformation of the raw material. The proportion of hoards containing a single category of artefacts rises from just over half the recorded material in Periods II, III and IV to 70 per cent in Period V and 84 per cent in Period VI. Over the same time, the proportion of ornament hoards rises sharply and the representation of tools and weapons decreases. As that happens, there are more finds associated with metalworking. The proportion of these 'metalworking hoards' rises from about 7 per cent in Periods II and III to approximately 17 per cent in Periods IV and V, before it falls to just 2 per cent at the end of the Bronze Age. Following Janet Levy's interpretation, this suggests that the earlier deposits were associated with men, women and smiths, whilst women provided more of the offerings towards the close of the period. At the same time, a higher proportion of the remaining material was associated with metalworkers and ritual specialists. There was little overlap between these different groups of finds, and during this sequence the number of deposits mixing weapons and ornaments fell from about 16 per cent of the total to only 2 per cent, suggesting that the roles played by these artefacts may have been more precisely defined.

This approach allows us to build on the analysis of find locations presented earlier in this chapter, which considered the relationship between the kinds of material being deposited and the places where that happened. Now we can also suggest the identity of some of the participants (see Table 2). There are obvious difficulties in taking this approach, and these have to be faced. The gender associations of these different artefacts must be extrapolated from the evidence of burials in other parts of Europe, and there is no way of demonstrating that the supposedly 'male' types were actually *deposited* by men or the 'female' associations by women, although that is a plausible hypothesis. Nor should we treat these patterns in isolation, for the decreasing representation of weaponry in southern Scandinavian hoards has to be viewed in a wider context. The number of supposedly female deposits certainly seems to rise during the later part of the Bronze Age, but this is just the time when the rock art of the same region includes numerous drawings of weapons, which are conventionally associated with men. Such drawings are mainly found in the eastern part of Sweden (Malmer 1981). Thomas Larsson has observed that the main groups of petroglyphs are found towards the edges of regions with metal finds, and he suggests that some of these images may have been regarded as another form of 'deposit' (1986: 139–58). In the west of Sweden and in south-west Norway, there are fewer carvings of weaponry but in this area the rock carvings contain a significant proportion of phallic humans (Malmer 1981). Again it seems as if rock art may have been associated mainly with men. Taking these observations together, it is not too much to suggest that over time 'hoarding' may have become a largely female domain,

Table 2 The changing associations of metal deposits in Bronze Age
          Denmark

Main location	Nature of deposit	Associations
Period II:		
Wet	Ornaments	Female
Wet	Weapons	Male
Dry	Tools	Smiths
Wet	Vehicle	Ritual specialist
Period IV:		
Wet and dry	Ornaments	Female
Dry	Scrap metal	Smith
Period V:		
Wet	Ornaments	Female
Wet	Weapons	Male
Wet	Scrap metal	Smith
Dry	Figurines, chains, clappers	Ritual specialist
Period VI:		
Wet	Ornaments	Female

Source: Levy 1982

whilst the imagery in the rock art of the same period had a predominantly masculine aspect. If so, the features of the natural landscape may have assumed their own gender associations. During the Later Bronze Age, the bogs in southern Scandinavia became female locations, whilst rock outcrops were regarded as male (Gibbs 1987).

Sunken vessels

The deposits mentioned earlier have been treated almost entirely in terms of the metalwork that they contain, but it is clear that on at least some sites the bronze artefacts were associated with other elements: human bones, animal bones and pottery. These have been overshadowed by archaeologists' interest in the metal finds, and sometimes the other material has not been recorded adequately. Yet comparison with the Saami votive deposits – the only ethnographic source of direct relevance to prehistoric Europe – suggests that the groups of metalwork were exceptional. Although they can be considered in more detail than any other finds, they must be seen in perspective, for, like the metal deposits of the Arctic, they seem to have resulted from the influx of exotic goods into an already established local system. How did that original system operate?

In order to consider a fuller range of deposits, it is necessary to turn to a period in which foreign metalwork was largely absent. Until recently this would have been difficult because the relevant material had not been studied in sufficient detail. Fortunately, this has been remedied by Eva Koch's study of the Neolithic pottery found in Danish bogs (Figure 15; Koch 1998 and 1999).

Again these deposits seem to have shared a characteristic type of location. They were placed close to the shore in what was open water at the time, often where a stream entered a lake or where two watercourses met. A number of the deposits were directly opposite an island or a conspicuous hill. There were megalithic tombs in the same area, and the bog deposits were not far from settlement sites and causewayed enclosures. Although they occupied a central position in the landscape, they were most closely related to the Neolithic hunting camps located on small islands, headlands or along streams. Where this is not apparent, they seem to have selected places that had been used in the Late Mesolithic, perhaps suggesting that these locations possessed an importance that extended into the past.

The biographies of these places are important too. The finds from the bogs have a lengthy history, and the earliest deposits may go back to the Ertebolle phase of the Late Mesolithic, when other artefacts from watery locations include flint axes, antler axes, amber beads, beads made from animal teeth, and shoe-last adzes imported from the area to the south. They occur in similar numbers in the earliest phases of the Neolithic, but they increased in frequency in parallel with the development of long barrows until there were deposits with pottery, axe heads and the bones of domesticated animals. The sequence in these places continued to mirror that on dry land. By the end of the Early Neolithic period, increasing quantities of artefacts were also associated with causewayed enclosures and

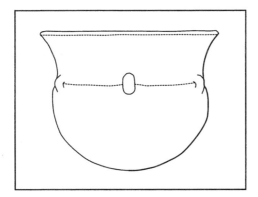

Figure 15 A Neolithic pot from the bog at
              Maglemose, Denmark
Source: Koch 1998

megalithic tombs. At the same time, the bog deposits became more extravagant and some of them were associated with wooden platforms. In addition to their usual contents, they included the bodies of sacrificed people and animals. After that time, pots were less often deposited in Danish bogs, but among the items that are found there are flint and greenstone axes, battle axes, beads, flint daggers, flint spearheads and the first copper axe heads. Some of these collections also contain human skulls.

Although such finds are related to those from the monuments on dry land, they are by no means identical to the material from these sites. The human remains are generally those of young people, although this was not the case in later periods, and the animal skeletons appear to result from sacrifices since there is no evidence that any meat was removed from the bone. The pottery has been compared with the large deposits in front of megalithic tombs, but it is surprisingly unvaried and lacks some of the more elaborate forms associated with those sites. The pottery found in the water had originally contained offerings of food, and its contents include the bones of domesticated animals, chaff, fish bones, fish scales and mast.

Although 30 per cent of the bogs with offerings of Neolithic pottery were used in only one phase, almost half the sites formed the focus for other deposits over a longer period of time, continuing in use in some instances as late as the Bronze and Iron Ages. Another 26 per cent of the bogs were reused after an interval or intervals in which there is no sign of similar activity. One of the most striking characteristics of these places is their extended history.

If some of the Bronze Age deposits resemble those associated with Classical sanctuaries, the Neolithic bog finds of Denmark have rather more in common with the sacrificial sites of the Arctic. Their operation seems to have been closely bound up with the success of the domestic economy, and this is supported by the presence of offerings of food and sacrificed animals. It was only as these practices developed that a wider range of artefacts came to be associated with these places. Until then, their siting in the landscape recalled the activities of the hunters who used the nearby camp sites and, further back, the landscape of the Ertebolle period when the first of these deposits were created. Their continuing significance was assured because the sites were so clearly marked by features like prominent hills.

Is the resemblance between these finds and Saami sacrificial deposits any more than coincidence? Some of the elements in Saami cosmology have been traced back to the Mesolithic period, and there is no doubt that similar beliefs were shared by hunters and herders across large areas of the Arctic, from Siberia to North America. Could some of those same ideas have had an even wider currency before the inhabitants of *southern* Scandinavia adopted the new ideology associated with communities across the agricultural frontier? Although most of the Danish bog finds are obviously linked to the use of domesticated resources, they seem to have originated before the adoption of farming and in areas that had already been important to hunter gatherers. They retained their link with hunting sites in the Neolithic period. The suggestion of a direct link with Saami ethnography is extremely tenuous, but, no matter how we explain it, this is yet another comparison that needs to be considered. Like the contents of the pots themselves, it provides food for thought.

Chapter 5

Seeing through stone

Rock art research as landscape archaeology

Rock art is characterised by the creation of particular images in particular places – it is not a uniform phenomenon. This chapter discusses the contribution of rock art research to landscape archaeology, and examines the connections between the choice of those images and their location in the terrain. It also considers the audience for the carved and painted designs, the accessibility – both physical and intellectual – of those images, their integration in the wider pattern of settlement and their treatment during later periods. In some respects the creation of these designs is rather similar to the provision of votive offerings. The chapter concludes with a discussion of the relationship between neighbouring styles of rock art in northern Iberia and southern Scandinavia. The contrasts between them epitomise many of the issues considered in this account.

Introduction

In Chapter 2 I quoted from Pausanias's account of the altars found in the countryside of Attica. Some of them seem to have been located in isolation at striking features of the topography such as mountain tops. They were an important element in the Classical landscape, but the same practices can also be identified in regions where they form part of a very different understanding of the world. Rather similar altars were raised in Roman Gaul, but in this case it is clear that they were located according to a long-established native cosmology.

Derks (1998) has recently studied this evidence and has drawn attention to those cult sites that lack any sign of monumental architecture. Some are evidenced by large numbers of votive offerings, but others include inscriptions and altars that can shed even more light on the significance of these locations. As he says, the majority of these places formed part of an indigenous mythical landscape, although they became assimilated into a wider system of belief.

The cult sites were often in the same kinds of places as those described by Pausanias. Derks emphasises the importance of several settings within the natural landscape. Among them were forests, hills and mountains, streams and rivers. The importance of these places was sometimes made clear by a dedication. For example, on top of the highest mountain in the northern Vosges there is a cult site with three reliefs depicting the Roman god Silvanus. It would not have been difficult to infer the importance of this mountain, but the association with Silvanus suggests that it was just as significant that the site was located in woodland. Elsewhere in the same region is a series of altars that suggest a similar association between the gods and the forest. Place names provide evidence for connections of much the same kind, and there are other cult sites whose names incorporate the Celtic element *nemeton*, which means a holy wood.

The link with watercourses is better documented, for in this case there are dedications to divinities who carry the same names as the local rivers. Among the locations that were especially favoured were confluences and crossing places. Springs were equally important. One site is particularly revealing in this respect, for at Kindsbach, beside the source of quite a minor river, there are stones carved with figures of the divinities, including Mars, Mercury and three seated goddesses, quite possibly the Matres. Derks suggests that one obvious association may be with rivers as a source of life.

This last site includes images that were carved from the living rock, a practice not confined to Gaul: a recent paper has drawn attention to a similar phenomenon in northern England (Charlton and Mitchelson 1983). This is especially interesting because 2,000 years earlier the same area had provided the setting for another group of carved stones, but in this case they were embellished by entirely abstract designs (Bradley 1997: Chapters 5 and 6). They cannot be interpreted through our knowledge of the Classical or native pantheon, yet both groups of images can properly be regarded as rock art.

This observation provides a useful starting point for discussion. Rock art can be characterised as the creation of visual images by painting or carving stone at particular places in the landscape. It is not a unitary phenomenon and it exhibits a wide range of variation across time and space. That is why it is legitimate to compare petroglyphs with free-standing sculptures and Roman inscriptions with entirely abstract designs. The element that connects them all is their association with unaltered features of the landscape, and in this respect they can be studied in much the same manner as votive deposits. That is not surprising, because these two phenomena are sometimes found together. We have already seen that this happens in Roman Gaul.

Once again it looks as if particular kinds of places may have been associated with specific powers or specific deities, but how were these places selected from the landscape as a whole? Is it possible to say why certain rocks were picked out for special treatment whilst others were left untouched? Were some types of outcrop especially favoured, and were any of these places marked by geological features that required interpretation? Is there evidence of a consistent relationship between particular kinds of location and particular kinds of images, just as the contents of different hoards seem to have been determined by the places in which they were deposited?

We have already seen how different kinds of offering might also be associated with separate parts of the population. What was the audience for prehistoric rock art? Were these designs accessible to everyone, or was access to the paintings and carvings restricted? If so, how was that restriction expressed? Certain images may have been located at remote places in the landscape, whilst others were easier to visit. Alternatively, certain motifs might be easier to interpret because they were naturalistic, whilst abstract designs posed greater problems of understanding. How were these places used? Were they associated with artefacts or other evidence of activities, or were the images created in apparent isolation? Most of these questions have to be answered by considering the place of rock art in the pattern of settlement.

Again, it is important to emphasise the sheer diversity of this phenomenon. None of these questions has just a single answer. Not only must we study rock art in relation to the wider landscape, but each image or group of images must be considered in its local cultural setting. The failure of more ambitious approaches has shown that this is not the kind of material that lends itself to too much generalisation.

The range of variation

Even if we limit ourselves to the rock art of the Neolithic and later periods, it is quite impossible to do justice to the full range of variation. Rather than attempting this, I prefer to approach each of these questions using a small number of well-documented examples. I shall then discuss the more impressive contrasts between two pairs of rock art styles, in Scandinavia and in Iberia. These may have been contemporary with one another.

Many different factors seem to have influenced the selection of particular surfaces as the sites for paintings or carvings. In western Norway, for example, rock paintings are found in caves at precisely the point of transition where the area that receives light from outside gives way to a zone that is entirely dark (Damm 1998). In northern Portugal, prehistoric paintings were often created on rocks that contained an unusual amount of natural quartz (L. Alves pers. comm.), whilst in Caceres in south-west Spain they were produced on surfaces with a striking natural colour: a reddish-yellow that does not occur widely in the surrounding area (García 1990). Similarly, rock carvings could be made in a variety of natural settings. Most of the petroglyphs in Britain and Ireland were on horizontal or gently sloping surfaces, where people could place offerings on the individual motifs (Figure 16), but a small number of unusual designs were carved on vertical surfaces where this procedure would have been impossible. Those designs have more in common with tomb decoration, and a special feature of these particular sites is that outcrops with carvings of spirals are normally red in colour: a characteristic that does not apply to most of the other petroglyphs (Bradley 1999). In southern Scandinavia, the Bronze Age rock carvings are usually on horizontal or sloping surfaces that had been smoothed by the passage of ice. They provide an ideal background for these images, yet in Bohuslän one of their most striking characteristics is that they are frequently covered by water flowing from the higher

Figure 16 Abstract cup and ring carvings at
Castleton, near Falkirk, Scotland

ground. Sometimes the rocks that were selected were unusually conspicuous ones, like a number of the carved outcrops in that area, whilst there are other cases where the more prominent outcrops were ignored in favour of less obvious loca- tions. A good example of that pattern is found in north-west Spain, where the Copper Age and Early Bronze Age carvings at Fentáns are on rocks that are difficult to identify from any distance away (Bradley *et al.* 1995), whilst two Roman inscriptions to the gods that occur in the same place are on top of massive outcrops (Santos *et al.* 1997). In the same way, fieldwork in north-east England has shown that the rocks with the most complex carvings are visible from more of the surrounding area than those with simpler designs (Bradley 1997: Table 13).

The detailed configuration of these rocks often played a part in the organisa- tion of the images. At Järrestad in southern Sweden, John Coles (1999) has shown that these were divided into distinct groups or panels formed by existing cracks in the surface of the stone. In western Norway, there are carved panels on vertical surfaces that incorporate pieces of natural quartz (Jan Magne Gjerde pers. comm.), whilst in Britain and Ireland wholly abstract designs may have been built up around geological features in the rock (Van Hoek 1997: 43–5). Natural pits or basins may have been embellished or enlarged, and sometimes they were enclosed by pecked lines and even joined to artificial features on other parts of the same outcrop. In certain cases, natural ripples visible in the surface of the rock resemble abstract carvings so strongly that these may have encouraged the 'artists' to add motifs of their own. We need to consider whether people in the past would have made a similar distinction. In northern Britain, there seems little doubt that individual panels of rock carvings were built up by the accretion of motifs over a long period of time. It is perfectly possible that what we can identify as natural features of these stones were regarded as still older carvings and imbued with special powers.

In the last chapter I suggested that different kinds of offerings were made in different kinds of places. A similar argument applies to the selection of painted and carved motifs employed in rock art. Some of these distinctions are very obvious indeed. In the north of Spain and Portugal, there are a number of paintings of people and animals found high up in the landscape, on cliffs and in caves and rock shelters. Some of these panels also include complex abstract designs. In the surrounding lowlands, there are numerous carvings of cup marks that may date from the same period (Sanches et al. 1998). A comparable distinction was observed in Scotland, where the fertile lowland areas contain a distribution mainly of cup marks and simple cups and rings, whilst more elaborate abstract designs overlook these areas (Bradley 1997: 101–4). By contrast, in Galicia, northern Spain, the most elaborate rock carvings are located in settlement areas and the cup marks are scattered across the uplands (Bradley et al. 1995). A similar distinction was observed in the west of Norway, where the more productive areas are characterised by complex naturalistic petroglyphs, whilst cup marks are concentrated on higher ground where some of the rocks would have been covered by snow for part of the year (Innselset 1995). Once again there is no reason to look for a uniform scheme. The important point is that in every one of these cases the nature of the carvings depended on their position in the wider terrain.

In fact, these distinctions may have applied across quite limited areas of the landscape and may even have cross-cut the distributions of individual 'styles'. Here the rock art of the southern Alps provides a useful example. Valcamonica is situated at the edge of the settled landscape and contains a mixture of abstract and naturalistic designs (Anati 1994). The same is true of Mont Bégo, which is located at a much greater height and would have been inaccessible in winter. In this case the range of motifs is much more limited, but they follow the same conventions (De Lumley 1995). At a third site, Carschenna, which was also located in summer pasture, there are few identifiable images and most of the carved panels are made up of abstract designs (Schwegler 1997). The distances involved are not great. Valcamonica is about 350 km (220 miles) from Mont Bégo and 150 km (95 miles) from Carschenna.

There is another point at issue here. Topographical variations may be reflected by differences among the painted and carved designs, but unless these were dedicated entirely to the supernatural, it is reasonable to think in terms of the audiences who would have seen them. Their siting is directly relevant here. Certain locations were within the margins of the settled landscape and would not have been difficult to find, although it is always possible that some people were *not allowed* to visit them. Among the regions where rock art is near to settlement sites are southern Scandinavia, southern Scotland, north-west Spain and northern Italy. In each case the locations of the rock carvings would have been obvious to everyone, and in some instances the rock outcrops themselves were conspicuous features of the local landscape. In Scotland and parts of northern England, for example, simple cup-marked rocks are found very close to the lithic scatters that seem to mark the positions of settlement sites (Bradley 1997: Chapter 6). In the same way, the more complex carvings in Galicia are around the edges of the well-drained basins that provided a major focus for domestic life during part of the year (Bradley *et al.* 1995). Others were located beside the paths that communicated between these places.

The local topography of these sites is important too. This is because so many of the images would have to be viewed from a particular perspective. For example, southern Scandinavian rock art included numerous drawings of people, animals and boats. All of these might be carved in relation to a single axis, so that the entire panel had to be seen from one direction. That was especially important where the surface of the rock shelved steeply. In such cases, it is clear that these sites were often in places that could accommodate quite a large audience (Nordbladh 1980). The same is certainly true of the naturalistic drawings found in Galician rock art, and is generally the case with the British and Irish petroglyphs, which were entirely abstract. In this case, there may be only one place from which all the motifs could be seen. Naturally, there are exceptions at some of the larger sites. As modern visitors to Achnabreck in western Scotland will be aware, only a selection of the carvings can be identified from the viewing platforms that have recently been installed on the site (Stevenson 1997). At the largest decorated rock in northern England, Roughting Linn, people would have needed to walk around the limits of the outcrop if they were to understand the entire range of images (Shee Twohig 1988); there is no physical impediment to prevent them from doing so.

That was not always the case. In other parts of Europe, the painted or carved surfaces might be more difficult to reach, and in this case it would certainly be possible to limit access to these images. For example, the rock carvings on Mont Bégo are located in the foothills of the Alps. Only shepherds and hunters would have encountered them in daily life, and in any case the images can have been accessible only during the summer months (Barfield and Chippindale 1997). The schematic art of northern Spain and Portugal is also located in quite remote parts of the uplands, where it can be difficult to find without the assistance of a guide. Some of the sites are fairly inaccessible and must be viewed by climbing mountains or working along the ledges on precipitous cliffs. No doubt people would become adept at moving between these places, but the painted caves and rock shelters could never have accommodated many individuals at the same time. Moreover, the paths leading to them are sometimes so steep and narrow that it would have been easy to prevent unauthorised people from seeing these sites (Bradley and Fábregas 1998). The clearest demonstration of this point is provided by the Abbé Breuil's publication of the later prehistoric rock art of Iberia (Breuil 1933–35). He was interested in the imagery and has little to say about their local setting, but his photographs speak for themselves. He never explains why there is often a ladder in the background.

To a certain extent, the local setting of these sites is reflected by the imagery that is found there. It is as if its character changed in relation to the audience who viewed it. This may be one way of accounting for the striking contrast between naturalistic styles of rock art and those that are entirely abstract.

I must make it clear what I do, and do not, mean by this suggestion. Certain images can be identified with features in the everyday world, such as people, animals and artefacts (Figure 17); other motifs cannot. On the other hand, rock art could probably be read at more than one level. The identification of those signs concerns only its *outer* meaning (Morphy 1991). It may be possible to recognise a particular drawing as a red deer, but what did the red deer signify to the people who depicted it? By contrast, a circle, a spiral or a row of dots does not copy anything taken from daily experience, and, because of that, they require more interpretation. They could be understood in many different ways, and knowledge of the right way in which to read those signs could only have been taught. Such knowledge might be offered or withheld. In neither case is it likely that a stranger would understand the entire meaning of a carved or painted panel. Even today,

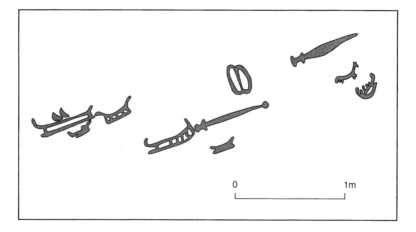

0   1m

Figure 17 Naturalistic rock carving at Himmelstadland, Ostergotland, Sweden
Source: Burenhult 1980

the same qualification applies to the Renaissance art displayed in public galleries. In prehistory, it may have been doubly difficult to interpret these designs in the appropriate manner. What people were allowed to know may have been determined by the nature of the audience for rock art and the occasions when the paintings and carvings were seen. Access to its significance could have depended on such features as age, gender and social status.

The distinction between naturalistic and abstract designs has a wider relevance (Figure 18). It seems as if abstract art is often associated with remote locations in the landscape, where few people could have seen these images at the same time. Naturalistic designs, on the other hand, tend to be found closer to the settlement sites, where the audience could have been very different (Bradley in press). The abstract designs overlap with those found in another specialised context – the chambers of megalithic tombs – whilst some of the naturalistic designs are shared with widely distributed styles of portable artefacts, in particular the Bronze Age metalwork of southern Scandinavia. Moreover, there is an important chronological pattern running through this material. Again, there are certain exceptions, but on the whole the earlier styles of rock art – those dating from the Neolithic – are largely or entirely abstract, whilst the groups that have been dated to the Bronze Age are mostly naturalistic.

It seems as if the traditions of painting and carving attributed to the Neolithic (and sometimes to the Copper Age) were dominated by images that could not be identified on the basis of everyday experience. Those images had something in common with the designs inside stone-built tombs and they are generally found on the margins of the settlement pattern or even beyond its limits. Among the places where they were created were cliffs, caves and rock shelters. The imagery itself is revealing, for some of the motifs bear a striking resemblance to those experienced in altered states of consciousness, brought on by intoxication, hallucination, hyperventilation and trance (Lewis Williams and Dowson 1988). Comparison with the ethnographic record suggests that certain of those images may record contacts with the supernatural experienced under these conditions. On the other hand, once such experiences had been notated in graphic form, they could have been copied and reinterpreted like any other text.

By contrast, the images that are chiefly dated to the Bronze Age (and in a few instances even to the Iron Age) recall features of the familiar world. This is not to suggest that these were pictures of daily life. No doubt these resemblances were relevant only to their 'outer' meaning. On the other hand, such compositions were more widely accessible than the others. They could have been created nearer to settlement sites, and some of the individual motifs had a still more general circulation through their use on portable artefacts.

I must stress again that there are styles of rock art that do not conform to that interpretation – the rock carvings of Britain and Ireland provide one notable exception – but for the most part it does seem as if those designs that were more accessible in physical terms were more accessible in intellectual terms as well.

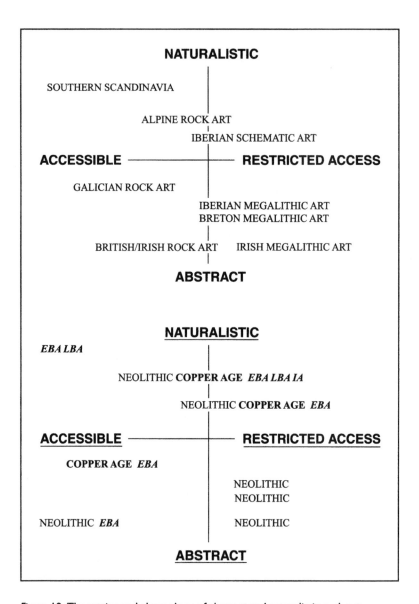

NATURALISTIC

SOUTHERN SCANDINAVIA

ALPINE ROCK ART

IBERIAN SCHEMATIC ART

ACCESSIBLE ——————— **RESTRICTED ACCESS**

GALICIAN ROCK ART

IBERIAN MEGALITHIC ART
BRETON MEGALITHIC ART

BRITISH/IRISH ROCK ART   IRISH MEGALITHIC ART

ABSTRACT

NATURALISTIC

EBA LBA

NEOLITHIC **COPPER AGE** *EBA LBA IA*

NEOLITHIC **COPPER AGE** *EBA*

ACCESSIBLE ——————— **RESTRICTED ACCESS**

COPPER AGE *EBA*

NEOLITHIC
NEOLITHIC

NEOLITHIC *EBA*   NEOLITHIC

ABSTRACT

Figure 18 The setting and chronology of abstract and naturalistic rock art

Note: The upper diagram summarises the locations of a series of major styles of rock art in relation to the character of their imagery and their position in the landscape. The lower diagram employs the same sample but substitutes their outline chronology.

Key: **EBA**: Early Bronze Age; **LBA**: Late Bronze Age; **IA**: Iron Age

Conversely, those that were hardest to reach were also more difficult to interpret. In neither case could they be understood without guidance, but where the rock art was completely abstract this would be especially difficult. The remote locations of the sites are reflected by the arcane character of the images that were made there, and in this case control over the meanings of the rock art may have been an important source of power (Bradley in press).

It is frustrating how little we know about the ways in which these places were used. There are sites where rock art seems to have been created in complete isolation and others that provided a focus for deposits of offerings or even burials. Unfortunately, these issues have not been investigated systematically because archaeologists have been more interested in the images than in their wider significance. No general patterns can be recognised at the moment, and what follows is a series of observations that relate to a few thoroughly investigated sites.

There are certainly cases in which rock art seems to have been created in complete isolation. Work on Passos/Santa Comba Mountain in northern Portugal suggests a striking difference between the contents of painted caves and rock shelters and those that were left undecorated. With only one exception, the caves with painted designs showed no trace of occupation and were virtually devoid of artefacts. By contrast, other caves in the vicinity did contain a significant number of finds, but these sites were entirely undecorated (Sanches 1997). The one exception was Buraco da Pala, an enormous cave just below the summit of the mountain which contained two small panels of painting. This cave was used over a long period, but seems to have played a very specialised role. It may have been employed for the storage and consumption of food, and in its filling was a range of specialised metalwork and even the carbonised seeds of opium poppies. The excavated assemblage is so distinctive that the site is interpreted as a sanctuary. Other painted caves and rock shelters in later prehistoric Iberia may have been used in much this way. The same applies to some of the carvings in southern Scandinavia, where there is evidence that platforms or small stone settings were created at the foot of the decorated surfaces (Johansen 1979). These were associated with large amounts of burnt stone, most probably from cooking, and with quantities of pottery that seem to have been broken and deposited at the base of the outcrop. In Britain, on the other hand, only one group of decorated rocks is associated with a deposit of artefacts (Edwards and Bradley 1999), and fieldwork at other sites has not produced any finds. The same is true in north-west Spain, where there is little evidence of artefacts in direct association with rock art. On the other hand, the groups of metalwork depicted in the carvings have the same composition as local weapon hoards. One of these was found near to a drawing of halberds and daggers, and another petroglyph was associated with a bronze axe (Bradley 1998b). Other artefacts were not found with the carvings themselves but do seem to have been placed among the rocks in the Galician landscape (Commendador 1995: 122–3).

Unlike hoards, rock art remains permanently visible. There is even more diversity in the later history of these places. Sites in Iberia were regularly reused. Some of those in Galicia saw the addition of further images after an interval of perhaps 1,500 years. These motifs are also found on funerary stelae of the Roman period (Santos *et al.* 1997). Something similar probably happened at the great hill fort of Yecla de Yelta in Salamanca, which seems to have been built on a site with an existing series of rock carvings, including drawings of animals that may date from the Early Bronze Age (Martin 1983). During the Roman Iron Age, fragments of these carvings appear to have been built into the defensive wall, whilst other animals were drawn in a quite different technique involving the use of a metal implement (personal observation 1995).

There was a further period of reuse during the medieval era, when large numbers of paintings and carvings in Iberia were embellished with Christian imagery (Martinez 1995). In some cases, these motifs were so similar to those made during the Copper Age that they have been difficult to tell apart (Costas 1998). These places were perhaps reused in reaction to the survival of traditional beliefs in the countryside. In the fifth century AD, the inhabitants of northern Portugal were specifically instructed to combat the pagan cult of rocks. Later, some of the decorated sites were reused by hermits, whilst others became foci for Christian pilgrimage (Sanches *et al.* 1998). Even when this did not happen, these places retained enough significance to be given names.

By contrast, there is little evidence of these processes in north-west Europe. In Britain and Ireland, in particular, very little attention was paid to the decorated surfaces until these sites had been publicised by antiquarians in the nineteenth century. Nor is there much evidence of Christian interest, except in a limited area around the pilgrimage site of Croagh Patrick in the west of Ireland (Corlett 1997). This may explain why the very existence of these sites had been forgotten. Hardly any of the carved rocks have their own names, and the people who own these places even today can be unaware of their significance. Because these sites contain an array of abstract motifs, the petroglyphs have sometimes been mistaken for features of the local geology.

Borderlands

The best way of encapsulating some of these variations is by comparing neighbouring styles of rock art with one another. I shall first consider the differences between Galician rock art and schematic art in the north of the Iberian peninsula and then the so-called hunters' and farmers' rock art of Scandinavia.

The first of these contrasts involves many of the issues that have been considered already. Although schematic art and Galician art had different histories, their chronologies seem to have overlapped during the Copper Age and the Early Bronze Age (Bradley and Fábregas 1998). Schematic art is a very general category, and the term is used to describe the painted and carved images found in most regions of Iberia apart from the Atlantic coastline. There are local variations within schematic art, picked out by the distribution of different kinds of motifs, but its vocabulary includes a mixture of naturalistic and abstract devices that extends from south-east Spain at one extreme to the north of Portugal at the other (Figure 19). Thus it provides a link between the Mediterranean world and the inland regions of Iberia.

Schematic art is entirely absent from the north-west, where its place is taken by Galician rock art (Figure 20); the occasional motifs that seem to suggest otherwise are probably of Christian origin. The term Galician art is something of a misnomer, since it is now known that similar designs can be found extending southwards for 150 km (95 miles) from the Spanish/Portuguese border (L. Alves pers. comm.). Even so, it remains a coastal phenomenon. If it has its counterparts in other areas, these are to be found in Britain, Ireland and perhaps in northern France. It is the abstract imagery that is most widely distributed, but at the heart of its distribution in the province of Pontevedra this is combined with drawings of animals and sometimes with depictions of weapons. Its repertoire has very little in common with that of megalithic art (García and Peña 1980).

Figure 19 Schematic art at Cueva de la Umbria del Canchal del
Cristo, Las Batuecas, Salamanca, Spain
Source: Breuil 1933

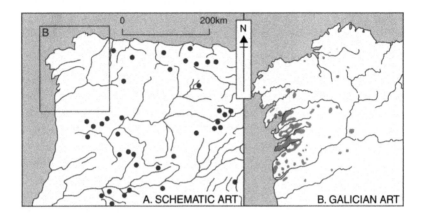

Figure 20 The distribution of schematic art and Galician rock art in northern Iberia

The two styles show a series of striking contrasts. Schematic art consists of paintings and carvings, and in the area where its distribution comes closest to that of Galician rock art it is usually found on the margins of the settled landscape. It tends to occur in striking and often quite inaccessible places, like cliffs or caves and rock shelters. The latter were not necessarily inhabited, although there can be occupied caves in the vicinity (Sanches 1997). The images were generally located on vertical surfaces and can be found in places where few people could have seen them at the same time. In the north of Portugal, their repertoire overlaps with that of megalithic art, suggesting that they may have possessed a special significance. There can be considerable variation within particular complexes, and it seems possible that some of the most elaborate paintings were created in the least hospitable locations. Such designs are sometimes found together with deposits of artefacts, but these can have a rather specialised character.

Galician rock art, on the other hand, was readily accessible and its distribution was closely linked to that of productive resources in the local landscape (Bradley *et al.* 1995). It extends from the coast into the higher ground, but is entirely confined to the parts of the landscape that were settled at the time. At a more detailed level, it is usually associated with sheltered and well-watered basins that could sustain occupation over a prolonged period or with the paths that communicated between these areas. The more complex panels were located close to these particular basins and often at the points where routes across the landscape led into them. Rather simpler motifs might also be found along these paths or where separate trails converged. In almost every case, the petroglyphs were created on inconspicuous rocks rather than on the more prominent granite outcrops in the same areas. The carved rocks commanded fairly limited views into the basins and along the tracks through the surrounding country. The only exceptions are carvings of stags with exaggerated antlers, which overlook the entire area from the higher ground (Santos 1998), and the depictions of weapons that occupy quite similar positions (Bradley 1998b). Although the weapon carvings can be on steeply sloping rocks, the remaining images normally occur on horizontal surfaces. As we have seen, very few of the rock carvings were associated with artefacts.

The two styles have overlapping histories and complementary distributions, yet they differ in almost every respect. Table 3 summarises the contrasts between them.

The other pairing is between the two main traditions of rock art in Scandinavia. These go under various names: hunters' art and farmers' art, Arctic rock art and south Scandinavian rock art, or, more simply, the Northern and Southern Traditions respectively. Their distributions are well known and overlap principally in the middle of Norway, but their chronological relationship is still contentious (Figure 21). The hunters' art obviously originated first, but most authorities allow for a period in which both styles were in use together. This account draws mainly on the work of Sognnes (1998).

Each style has its characteristic repertoire. The Northern Tradition is mainly associated with drawings of wild animals, including reindeer, red deer and elk, as well as birds, fish and whales. Some of their bodies are infilled by abstract motifs that have features in common with the entoptic imagery experienced during altered states of consciousness (Lewis Williams and Dowson 1988). By contrast, the farmers' art of the Southern Tradition is mainly exemplified by boats and footprints as well as many cup marks. The art of the Northern Tradition includes both paintings and carvings; the Southern Tradition is limited to petroglyphs. The two styles overlap in an area that was towards the agricultural frontier around 2500 BC. In a later phase, this was the region in which the material culture of the Nordic Bronze Age came into contact with a separate tradition whose wider associations extended to Finland and, across the Baltic, to the former Soviet Union (Kristiansen 1998: 70–1).

Both groups of carvings can be found close to settlement sites, but their locations are quite different from one another. The hunters' art was located on the shoreline. It favoured conspicuous positions in the landscape, some of

Table 3 The contrasting attributes of schematic and Galician rock art in northern Iberia

Attribute	Schematic art	Galician rock art
Position in the landscape	Marginal	Central
Ease of access	Difficult	Easy
Media	Painting and carving	Carving
Decorated surfaces	Mainly vertical	Mainly horizontal
Associated artefacts	Quite common	Very rare
Relations to tomb art	Significant overlap	Little overlap
Contexts of use	Specialised, ritual	Regular, domestic

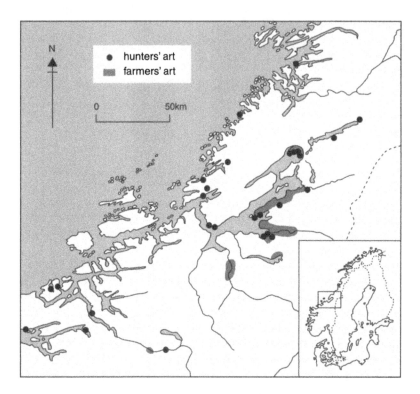

Figure 21 The distribution of hunters' art and farmers' art in western Norway
Source: Sognnes 1998

which were visible from one another, but, as Sognnes says, 'rock art [was] not found at the top of these prominent locations but near their lower edges, often facing the sea' (1998: 154). These places were probably not used as hunting stands but were distributed along the trails followed by wild animals. They have been interpreted as sanctuaries. The farmers' art, on the other hand, covered more of the landscape and could often be located some way inland. The groups of rock carvings were located at intervals of approximately 2 km (1 mile) and were equally spaced. They do not occupy particularly prominent positions and can be recognised only from nearby. 'The rock art sanctuaries were located at the dwelling sites, out of sight and reach from travellers' (Sognnes 1998: 157).

Again, we can observe a series of striking contrasts between two styles of rock art whose histories overlapped. In this case, that was also true of their distributions. Some of these contrasts, as shown in Table 4, recall the evidence from Iberia, but others are quite different. They illustrate the sheer diversity of rock art, even in one small area.

Table 4 The contrasting attributes of hunters' art and farmers' art in western
Norway

Attribute	Hunters' art	Farmers' art
Position in the ladnscape	Conspicuous	Inconspicuous
Media	Painting and carving	Carving
Imagery	Naturalistic, abstract	Naturalistic
Contexts of use	Specialised	Domestic

Conclusion

In many ways, the places with rock art are similar to those with hoards. In each
case, a particular location has been selected from the wider landscape and used in
a special way. With hoards or votive deposits, particular groups of offerings were
made in particular places. In the case of rock art, it seems as if specific kinds of
location were associated with appropriate images. These relationships may relate
to the different kinds of beliefs associated with these sites. At the same time, much
may have depended on the people who made use of these places. In Chapter 4 we
saw how different groups may have provided quite separate kinds of offering. The
same is true of the painted and carved motifs, the choice of which may reflect the
identity of those who made them and the character of the audiences to whom
they were addressed. In view of these striking similarities, it is not so surprising
that the carvings of metalwork found in Scotland and northern Spain should
portray the same combinations of artefacts as we find in local hoards (Bradley
1998b).

This chapter has treated rock art as part of a wider archaeology of natural
places, and has considered some of the ways in which it can be integrated into
interpretations of the ancient landscape. But one problem still remains. Again,
this is a question that also applies to the locations chosen for the votive deposits
studied in Chapter 4. Rock art is identified by the marking of places with signs,
whereas hoards were identified through the offerings that were deposited there. In
both cases, the significance of a particular location becomes archaeologically
identifiable through that activity, and yet there is every reason to think that the
place itself had achieved a special significance before either of these events
occurred. Among the Saami, for example, particular rocks did not achieve their
significance because offerings had been made there. Rather, those places were
selected because their natural topography resembled the form of a living creature,
often a god. The altars erected in the countryside of Roman Gaul were often
placed there because particular spots already played a role in the mythical landscape, yet it is a role that can be grasped only in those rare instances where a place
name survives. There is an inevitable tension between the kinds of phenomena
that we are investigating and the procedures of field archaeology, and as a result

we are able to recognise only parts of what was once a much wider pattern. Fortunately, we are free to make this attempt in many different ways. Having considered the contribution of rock art research in this chapter, we shall now turn our attention to the study of production sites.

Chapter 6

The movement of mountains

Production sites and the archaeology
of places

This chapter discusses the production and distribution of Neolithic artefacts
from a new perspective. Rather than laying an emphasis on technology and
exchange, it considers the qualities attached to the places where those objects
were made and the ways in which they took on some of that significance. This
process is reflected by the unusual manner in which such items were treated.
There is a continuum from the making of artefacts to the use of raw materials in
purely ceremonial roles. The discussion extends from stone axe production to the
introduction of raw materials to Irish passage graves, and concludes with a new
interpretation of the bluestones at Stonehenge.

Pieces of places

Chapter 4 was a study of votive deposits and Chapter 5 was concerned with rock
art. On the west coast of Norway, both these elements are combined with the
evidence from axe production sites.

Two groups of rock art are exceptionally important here. These occur at Ausevik and Vingen, both of which are located on the coastline (Figure 22). The dates
of these sites are controversial, but Vingen may have originated during the Mesolithic period, whilst some authorities prefer a Neolithic context for Ausevik (Mandt
1995). They are characterised by abstract motifs but also by a large number of
drawings of animals, some of which may include entoptic imagery. Vingen is
located in a particularly impressive natural setting and the site is difficult to reach.

> The tiny fjord, surrounded by steep and seemingly impassable mountains,
> with its large number of rock pictures gives the impression of a very special –
> even a sacred – place. The view from Vingen towards a characteristic moun-
> tain formation called Homelen adds to this impression. . . . A variety of
> legends and stories are associated with this mountain.
>
> (Mandt 1995: 278)

The coastal part of western Norway was densely settled during the period in
which these images seem to have been created, but the inland areas were not used

Figure 22 The natural setting of the rock art complex at Vingen, western Norway
Source: Trond Lødøen

as intensively. It is here that a number of Mesolithic axe heads have been found. A detailed examination of these finds by Lødøen (1998) suggests that they had not been lost by chance. Excavation shows that they were not associated with settlement sites and in fact were generally found in a small number of distinctive contexts, in streams, in screes or associated with large stones. More than one example was discovered in some of these locations, leading Lødøen to conclude that these were probably votive deposits.

Stone axes of this kind were made at two major sites on the coast: Hespriholmen and Stakaneset (Figure 23). These were used in both the Mesolithic and Neolithic phases, and their products have mutually exclusive distributions, suggesting that they may have been worked by different communities (Bruen Olsen and Alasker 1984). This idea is supported by studies of how other raw materials were used during the Neolithic period (Knut Andreas Bergsvik pers. comm.).

As we have seen, there is a convincing case that axe heads of this kind were used as votive deposits in inland areas. That makes it particularly important to investigate the circumstances in which these artefacts were made. Here all three categories of evidence come together, for each of the quarries is located near to important groups of rock art. Vingen and Ausevik are not far away from the large diabase quarry at Stakaneset, whilst there are other rock carvings close to the major stone source at Hespriholmen. This has led to the suggestion that the two types of site might be linked. Perhaps the concentrations of rock art represent

Figure 23 The location of the stone axe quarry at
          Stakaneset, western Norway
Source: Knut Andreas Bergsvik

ceremonial centres in special locations close to the sources of these stones (Bruen Olsen and Alasker 1984).

The quarries take on an added significance in the light of these suggestions, for each is a striking field monument in its own right. The greenstone quarry at Hespriholmen is located on a small exposed island some distance off the coast, whilst diabase axes were made at Stakaneset on a massive cliff that projects into the sea (Alasker 1987). Both are exposed to the extreme weather found on the coast, and, as Lødøen (1998) says, this makes access to the sites difficult and even dangerous. There is no doubt that they provided good-quality stone, but might some of the importance attached to the axes produced there result from the circumstances in which they were made? This is especially important in view of the rock art found in the same region.

A similar argument applies to the archaeology of northern Norway. Here there is a major complex of rock art, located at the coast on Alta Fjord (Helsgog 1988). Despite its characteristic siting, some of the imagery is related to land animals, especially in the third phase of activity at the site, which is dated to 2700–1700 BC. This may be related to increasing use of the interior at this time. That suggestion takes on an added significance with the discovery of no fewer than three separate quarry sites, all of them within 7.5 km (4½ miles) of the carvings. They were important sources of chert for use over a larger area (Hood 1988).

It seems as if both phenomena were related to one another in the same way as the rock art at Ausevik and Vingen may have been linked with the production of stone axes. Bryan Hood has suggested that the rock carvings at Alta were a major source of sacred knowledge, access to which could have been controlled. That control might have been of two kinds. There is the question of purely physical access to the carved surfaces themselves, but the meanings of those images might also have been protected, so that their full significance would have been revealed only to certain people. Hood compares the role of the Alta rock art as a 'fixed' source of information with that of the chert obtained nearby, which had a wide distribution in Finmark. Perhaps this was not just a serviceable raw material:

> Chert sources . . . articulated with the rock carvings and the social relations they legitimated through a common ideological structure, but they did so in a complementary rather than identical manner. While . . . information – carvings – was engraved *into* the bedrock that constituted an ideologically charged point in the natural and social geography, requiring the movement of otherwise spatially distant consumers to read the messages, another kind of information – chert – was riven *out* of that same bedrock . . . and transported to distant points in the social geographic network where it carried a more restricted message. . . . Chert acted as a mnemonic for the interaction system without providing the running commentary on social relations that was encoded in the carvings.
>
> (Hood 1988: 78)

Thus the chert was not simply a useful raw material, although that was certainly the case. Its acquisition and exchange bound communities living in inland areas into the wider system of belief associated with the great concentration of rock carvings on the coast, and testified to their involvement in that wider world.

It is a model that may have a wider application, for artefacts are not simply instruments for adaptation, they may also carry associations with the places where they were made. This chapter explores that possibility through a variety of case studies taken from the Neolithic and Early Bronze Age periods. To keep the subject within bounds, the discussion is limited to stone sources, but similar arguments could as easily be devoted to the use of metals. Its aim is to locate these sources and their use within the archaeology of the wider landscape. The examples explored in detail suggest that there is a continuum from the use of particular raw materials to produce artefacts for exchange to the incorporation of different stone types in megalithic monuments. The discussion begins with another quarry site.

Artefacts as places

The existence of Neolithic axe quarries in the Langdale Fells of north-west England had been postulated for a long time before the sites were located. Work began when geologists studied the composition of stone axes and suggested that some of them had originated in this area. Their analysis was followed by the discovery of a few production sites (Bunch and Fell 1949), but it was not for another forty years that these places were surveyed in detail (Claris and Quartermaine 1989). Until then there was considerable confusion as to where those artefacts were made.

That confusion is revealing. In public perception, the production site was an enormous scree extending for the full height of the conspicuous mountain known as Pike o' Stickle (Figure 24). It is identified as an 'axe factory' in the local guidebooks, and in recent years it has suffered from the attention of collectors. Professional archaeologists often experienced the same confusion. They were aware that 'Cumbrian' axes originated from this area, but they were uncertain how or where they were made. That was because the production sites themselves – the origin of the debris flowing down the mountainside – were located in such inaccessible places. The problem was not that they were unrecognisable. On the contrary, some of the quarries are most impressive field monuments (Claris and Quartermaine 1989). Rather, it seemed unthinkable that such a productive industry could operate from such remote locations. The very idea seemed inconsistent

Figure 24 The location of the stone axe quarries at Pike o' Stickle, Cumbria, north-west England; the quarries were located above the scree on the steep flank of the mountain

with the large number of artefacts that were made there and with their wider distribution across the country. Indeed, a number of the products were taken across the Irish Sea where no fewer than 43 per cent of them were deposited in rivers and bogs (Cooney and Mandal 1998: Chapter 5).

Such uncertainty was understandable because of the very assumptions that archaeologists brought to production sites of this kind. There was much discussion of 'efficiency' (Torrence 1986). How proficient were the techniques by which the rock was worked? How much of the raw material was wasted? It seemed important to discuss the practicalities of reaching the stone source and the best ways of removing artefacts from the site. Underlying all these questions was the Principle of Least Effort (Zipf 1949). Prehistoric people were supposed to have calculated how they might maximise output while minimising labour. The identification of the quarry sites at Langdale showed that this approach was misleading.

Although workable stone occurs along an exposure that runs for 19 km (12 miles), it was not used throughout its distribution (Bradley and Edmonds 1993: Chapters 4–7). Some outcrops were exploited by shallow surface workings, but the quarries that provided most of the raw material were on narrow ledges high up on the face of Pike o' Stickle, in locations that were both difficult and dangerous to reach. On the other hand, they commanded enormous views. Taken together, the production sites are among the most remote archaeological monuments anywhere in England. Indeed, those on Scafell Pike, 5 km (3 miles) from Pike o' Stickle, are within a short distance of the highest point in the country.

Oddly enough, fieldwork on these remarkable quarries happened at the same time as articles appeared questioning the importance of extraction sites of this kind. In one case, these doubts were based on the techniques by which particular artefacts had been assigned to specific source areas; certain axes might not have been made together, whilst others could have been produced in more than one locality (Berridge 1993). More revealing was an attempt to show that the great majority of Neolithic axe heads in Britain were made from glacial erratics (Briggs 1989). If this were so, it would certainly reduce the significance of formal quarries. It would also undermine the argument that the products of those sites were distributed over large areas. It is true that a system of this kind might have been more 'cost-effective', and that by substituting geological factors for human agency it would be possible to question the importance of exchange systems during the Neolithic period. But that is not what the evidence shows.

In fact, new studies of stone axe production have only emphasised the sheer complexity of this process. In doing so, they have also highlighted the distinctive character of the places where these artefacts were made. There have been three important developments. First, new work at Langdale has served to emphasise the special character of the place itself. A study of the rock outcrops, employing the principles of materials science, shows that some of the most suitable stone for making work tools was left unused, whilst inaccessible exposures with the same physical characteristics were employed instead (Bradley *et al.* 1992). The character of the place seemed at least as important as the qualities of the material that was found there. Moreover, a survey of the entire distribution of the parent rock shows that, contrary to the Principle of Least Effort, people chose to quarry the stone in precisely those areas that were located furthest from the lower ground. They also selected quarry sites overlooking the steepest gradients. In each case, the effect was the same, for it helped to isolate these places from the sphere of everyday activity (Watson 1995).

A second development is the investigation of more quarry sites. These included two examples on islands: Rathlin Island off the coast of Ulster and Lambay Island near to Dublin. The evidence from Rathlin Island is especially important here as this site is difficult to reach in bad weather. The journey involves a dangerous sea crossing. The stone that was obtained there was obviously more than was needed to supply the local inhabitants, and yet it is virtually indistinguishable from the rock that was quarried on a more extensive scale at Tievebulleagh on the mainland. Both were the source of axes of similar type. In common with the principal sites in Cumbria, the most distinctive feature of Rathlin Island was its remote location (Williams 1990). The same is true of the recently discovered axe quarries on Lambay Island, and here excavation has produced convincing evidence for rituals taking place at the stone source that are very similar to those recognised at monuments of Neolithic date (Cooney 1998).

The third development concerns the use of glacially derived stone. It has long been recognised that stone axes were also made out of rock that occurred in the Preseli Hills in south-west Wales, but the sources had never been identified on the ground. Recent work has shown that at least some of these artefacts were made from boulders of the same raw material, obtained from nearby deposits of glacial till. Any attempt to provide a purely 'rational' explanation for this practice is undermined by the discovery that the production area included a small ceremonial monument, albeit of uncertain date (David and Williams 1995). Thus even when the stone came from more accessible locations, its transformation may have been attended by special rituals. Again, an entirely practical interpretation seems to be excluded.

These results lend weight to a more subjective impression. It is clear that the locations selected for axe quarries often stand out from the surrounding country because of their unusual physical characteristics. This is a difficult question to discuss because there is such a danger of imposing modern aesthetics on the past, but it is certainly true that sites like Pike o' Stickle, Graig Lwyd, Creag na Caillich and Le Pinnacle dominate the surrounding landscape. A number of them can be seen from an enormous distance away. The Langdale Pikes, for instance, can be distinguished from all the other mountains on the Lake District skyline. In some cases, there is environmental evidence to confirm that this would have been true in the past, as these places seem to have been on, or even above, the tree line.

The evidence from British and Irish axe production sites is limited but consistent. They were often located in spectacular but unusually inaccessible places, where the individual quarries would be difficult to find by chance. For the most part they were located well beyond the limits of the settled landscape in areas that might be hazardous to reach. It would have been just as difficult to remove the artefacts produced there. As often as not, work tools could have been made from other exposures of the same raw material without experiencing any of these hardships.

At the same time, it has long been accepted that the movement of the finished products across country cannot have been governed entirely by practical considerations. Certain rock types were preferred to others, even in areas with adequate raw materials of their own. Axes made out of easily recognisable rocks were treated differently from the products of other stone sources, and might be committed to the ground with some formality in graves, hoards, rivers or pits (Bradley and Edmonds 1993). Moreover, the techniques of materials science show that on a national scale some of the most suitable materials for axe making were underexploited, compared with other kinds of stone (Bradley *et al.* 1992). Those that were preferred generally came from unusual locations. The people who acquired these axes at a distance from their source obviously understood these connotations. Such objects were not only artefacts with a history of their own: this evidence suggests that they might have been considered as 'pieces of places'.

Flint mines were another source of raw material for making axes, but again their interpretation is far from straightforward. To some extent, this is because mining took place during a period when pits and shafts of other kinds played a significant role in ritual life in Britain. Many monuments contained settings of deep pits, but others exist in apparent isolation. Some of these had been excavated by the same techniques as the mines, whilst others were most likely of natural origin. For example, a deep shaft, almost certainly the result of chemical solution, is found just beside the Dorset Cursus (Green and Allen 1997). This seems to have provided the focus for a series of placed deposits extending throughout the Neolithic and ending only when the site was capped by a deposit of rammed chalk during the Beaker period. Not far away is a similar shaft, located near to the original terminal of the Cursus. This was an entirely artificial construction, dug at virtually the same time as that monument was built. At its base were a series of pig bones and a large block of chalk decorated in a style that resembles megalithic art (Martin Green pers. comm.).

Both of the sites are on the Wessex downland where flint mines would have been familiar, but there is similar evidence from other parts of the country. In this case, the shafts seem to have formed naturally, although this distinction might not have been apparent to people in the Neolithic, just as it has confused field archaeologists to the present day. At Eaton Heath near Norwich, a series of these features occurred on what may have been a settlement site. Several of them contained complete vessels of Neolithic pottery of a kind that might otherwise have been buried in shallow pits (Wainwright 1973). Shafts of rather similar type can be formed in limestone. Again, these were features of the local geology, yet they were used for the deposition of human remains (Hayes 1987). Some of the solution holes on the Mendips are found close to small henge monuments (Figure 25; Stanton 1986).

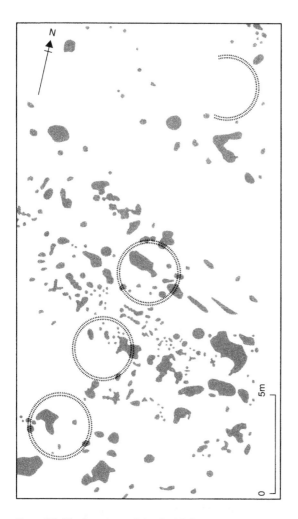

Figure 25 The locations of the Priddy henge monuments,
            Somerset, England, in relation to the
            distribution of natural sinkholes in the
            limestone
Source: Information from Stanton 1986

These arguments suggest a new perspective on British flint mines, which have
been interpreted in much the same way as the axe quarries. It has always been
supposed that they played a central role in Neolithic adaptations to the natural
environment: good-quality flint was extracted to provide axes for clearing the
landscape. This was not always true. In many regions, perfectly adequate flint
could be – and was – obtained with much less effort from surface exposures of

clay with flints overlying the chalk or from the flint seams exposed in natural cliffs (Gardiner 1990). Moreover, flint mining was an extremely wasteful business, and it does not seem as if the most efficient use was made of the raw material. In some cases, little of this was worked. Indeed, a feature that links some of the mid-Sussex mines with one of the opencast quarries at Great Langdale is the way in which the rejected raw material was apparently reused for tool making during a later period. Indeed, it is unclear that axes were always the main product of these sites.

Many of the British flint mines complemented the use of other surface deposits where the same kinds of artefacts were made. Again, that may be true of the Neolithic stone quarries in highland Britain. The main characteristic that they have in common is their remote location (Edmonds 1995: Chapters 3 and 4). Just as sites like Langdale were located well outside the areas of year-round settlement, the main flint mines in Sussex and Wessex are offset from the distribution of long barrows and earthwork enclosures dating from the same period. They also avoid the distribution of settlement sites, as evidenced by dated flint scatters. That is particularly interesting because it was in those areas that greater use was made of surface exposures.

In fact, the source of the raw material may have been as important as its mechanical performance. It may have gained in value because of the hazards involved in its acquisition; and knowledge of the place where an artefact was made may have mattered as much as its ostensible function. When we consider that the flint had been extracted from deep and dangerous mines, there is much in common between this interpretation and the interpretation of Great Langdale.

Continental scholars acknowledge the importance of the same considerations. In her account of raw material extraction in Bavaria, Marjorie De Grooth comments on the laborious extraction of chert from the mines at Arnhofen. This is perplexing because it has no obvious features that would explain why it was used. Its main feature is its distinctive appearance, which would have been sufficient to inform people of where it was obtained (De Grooth 1997). In the same way, Elisabeth Rudebeck (1998) has described the way in which axes made in the Neolithic flint mines of Scania were characterised by a small area of cortex that was left when the remainder of the raw material was worked. Again, she suggests that what mattered was that the original source of these objects could be recognised. It was important that it should be understood that they had come from mines. They had an added importance because they originated in remote places deep underground.

Placing the dead

I have already commented on the way in which the study of flint mines and axe quarries had emphasised pragmatic considerations: the mines were an efficient way of obtaining high-quality work tools, whilst quarrying was managed according to the Principle of Least Effort. I also summarised the argument that most axe heads were produced from locally available erratics. What these approaches have in common is an insistence on applying a modern, western logic to the societies of the past. The assumptions that they make are those of the contemporary economy: that goods should be produced with the smallest amount of labour and the greatest potential profit. That approach is concerned with minimising risk and maximising output. It could only have been proposed at a time when archaeologists themselves had become obsessed with management.

That approach to the past is especially difficult to apply to sites like megalithic tombs. In some cases, the material used in building these monuments was obtained on the spot, but in others it had been collected over some distance and emphasised such features as the colour and composition of the rock. This was the situation on the north Wessex downs around Avebury, where a number of long barrows and megalithic tombs have been investigated. The major structural components of these monuments consist of large pieces of sarsen that could have been obtained locally, on the Marlborough Downs. They provided the main structural supports for the monuments, but may themselves have possessed an added significance, for two of the sarsens incorporated into West Kennet long barrow had been used for polishing axes, whilst another axe-polishing stone still remains in its original position on Overton Down nearby (Piggott 1962: 19). On the other hand, this does not explain why the locally available stone should have been supplemented by much smaller pieces of oolite, which had been introduced to these sites from 25 km (15½ miles) away (Smith 1965: 117–18). These stones added nothing to the structural stability of the tombs and did not even play a conspicuous part in their design.

The problem is particularly obvious when we recognise that stones from the same source were found in the causewayed enclosure on Windmill Hill, where they do not seem to have been used as artefacts. On the other hand, the excavated material from that enclosure does include a large amount of pottery imported from the same area. This is evident because rock of identical type had been used as filler in the clay (Smith 1965: 44). It seems quite possible that both were brought to the Avebury area together, but why should pieces of apparently nondescript stone have been employed in the same manner as artefacts? I suggest that this happened because of a feature of this material that we too easily take for granted. The body of the pots includes fossil shell. This imparted a certain mechanical efficiency, but it may be at least as interesting that these fragments could be recognised as the remains of living creatures. Perhaps it was the fact that the rocks contained traces of these life forms that made it so important to incorporate them in artefacts and megalithic tombs; the same applies to the occasional use of bone tempering in the pottery found at such monuments in the Cotswolds and the west of Ireland (Hulthén 1984; Saville 1990: 146). Artefacts of this kind might express links with other places, but they could also have formed connections with the past.

A very similar process is apparent in the Boyne Valley, where deposits of unworked boulders have been discovered during excavation of the passage graves at Newgrange and Knowth. These are chiefly concentrated in front of the entrances to the tombs, although some examples may have been used to enhance the surface of the mounds. They come from a very wide range of natural sources, many of them from beaches along the shoreline of the Irish Sea. The distribution of this material extends across an area from Carlingford Lough to the north as far as the Wicklow Mountains, 75 km (46 ½ miles) to the south (Mitchell 1992). It is important to stress that very few of the boulders could have played any practical role in the construction of the tombs. They are simply natural stones brought to the sites and deposited outside the entrance of these monuments. Like the axe heads that are found there, they can be interpreted as offerings, but they are entirely unmodified and were not functional artefacts at all. Rather, they evoke connections between the monuments of the Boyne Valley and a variety of natural places in the wider landscape. Perhaps the same process explains why deposits of seashells should have been found in similar structures up to 60 km (37 miles) inland from the coast (Herity 1974: 173).

The most important of these stones is undoubtedly the quartz, which was brought to the Boyne Valley from the Wicklow Mountains. Its precise role is controversial. It is found at the main mounds at Newgrange and Knowth. The excavator of Newgrange considered that a massive deposit of quartz flanking the entrance to the tomb represented the remains of a revetment wall (O'Kelly 1982: Chapter 5), but it is doubtful whether this would have been structurally stable. Perhaps this material was simply used to enhance the exterior of the mound. Whatever the reason, one point is very clear: the stones were brought in quantity from the mountains to a series of chambered tombs situated in a river valley. Newgrange and Knowth are among the largest passage graves in Ireland, but they differ from many of the others in their lowland setting (Herity 1974: Chapter 2). Perhaps the selection of raw material from that particular source helped to evoke connections with the mountains where such structures are more often found.

That example is unusual because it has always been accepted that these patterns were archaeologically significant. This has not been the case with the bluestones at Stonehenge, for here opinion has oscillated between the deliberate acquisition of exotic raw materials for use in this great monument, and their movement by melting ice (Thorpe et al. 1991). At present, the traditional view seems to receive most support (Green 1997; Scourse 1997), and in the absence of any strong evidence to the contrary it is the interpretation that I shall follow here.

There are two important points to recognise in considering the use of raw materials in Stonehenge. Some of the stone, the sarsen, is of quite local derivation, whilst the remainder seems to originate in south-west Wales. Although it had its sources in the Preseli Hills, it does not come from a single deposit, but consists of a number of different rock types that could all be obtained within the same region (Figure 26).

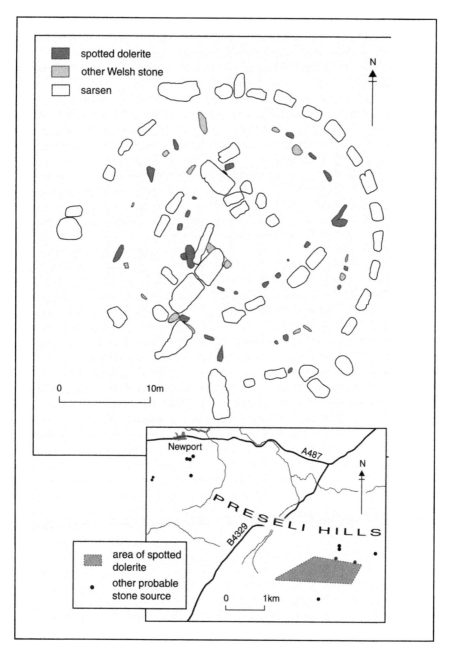

Figure 26 The geological identification of the rocks used at Stonehenge, and an outline map
of the source area of the bluestones in south-west Wales
Source: Information from Thorpe *et al.* 1991

Both these distinctions were appreciated by the builders of the monument. None of the structural features of Stonehenge was designed to mix material from the two main source areas, nor were all the bluestones used together – at least in the parts of the monument that have survived to the present day. Rather, the full range of non-local stone types was employed in an outer ring of bluestones, whilst the inner setting consisted of spotted dolerite (Cleal *et al.* 1995: Figure 15). Clearly, the distinctions between the different stone types were considered to be important. At the centre of the inner setting is the so-called Altar Stone, the only piece of green sandstone used in the monument. The bluestones were significant in another way, for, unlike the sarsens on the site, they were regularly used as a source of artefacts. As we have seen, rock from the Preseli Hills was also used to make axes. At Stonehenge we find fragments of partly worked bluestone that resemble axe roughouts, but these were apparently made *on the site itself* (Cleal *et al.* 1995: 380). This suggests that the different forms of stone transport were regarded as comparable processes.

There are many inponderables – the bluestones may have been introduced to Wessex long before they were used at Stonehenge; they could have been the remains of a dismantled monument taken from another site – but the simplest hypothesis is that they were brought direct to Stonehenge. What is clear is that the local raw material remained in position once it had been erected, whereas the bluestones were installed and taken down again on as many as three occasions (Cleal *et al.* 1995: Chapter 7). They seem to have been employed in the first stone setting on the site, but this structure was dismantled when the sarsen trilithons were built. Thus the bluestones could have been considered as the oldest material in the monument, as well as the most exotic. Their antiquity would have been enhanced during later phases, when a second stone setting seems to have been dismantled. Now they bore obvious traces of their earlier history, for some had been carefully dressed whilst others carried the remains of joints that had held a lintelled structure together (Cleal *et al.* 1995: Figure 116).

Stonehenge is a unique monument yet it is securely grounded in the local landscape. On one level, its extraordinary history makes most sense in relation to the long-distance networks that characterise the Late Neolithic and Early Bronze Age periods. These are exemplified by the wide range of artefacts found in the surrounding area. At the same time, the stone building was the immediate successor of a timber circle, and that in turn replaced a causewayed enclosure (Cleal *et al.* 1995: Chapter 10). Each of these monuments has its counterparts elsewhere in the same region. These two strands in the history of Stonehenge are aptly symbolised by the choice of raw materials for building the final monument: gigantic sarsens of quite local derivation that recalled the less sophisticated structures at Avebury; and the bluestones themselves with their links with the Preseli Hills and with the flow of non-local axes across the country as a whole. One set of materials referred to a striking feature of the Wessex landscape – the extensive spreads of sarsens on the downland – whilst the other referred to a series of spectacular landforms that few people might have seen (Figure 27). The finished structure at

Figure 27 One of the distinctive formations on Carn Meini, south-west Wales; the rock divides into a series of natural columns resembling a megalithic structure and provided a major source of raw material for Stonehenge

Stonehenge (if it ever was finished) achieved a precarious balance between the two. In the earliest stone circle, the bluestones stood on their own, but in every succeeding phase they were enveloped by a more massive ring of local materials. As the history of the monument lengthened, they came to stand not just for the exotic and remote but also for the past itself. Now they were relics taken from a remote and spectacular landscape but they were also the tangible remains of older structures on the site and with each new rebuilding they bore the mark of an even longer period of use. In the end they were enveloped by an enclosure of enormous proportions in which the fragments of the original building were dwarfed by the settings of sarsen. Even then, the various categories of Welsh rock were separated from one another in the structure of the monument, *for the sources of the different stones were still important after 500 years.* It is impossible to interpret the significance of all these changes, but they seem to be concerned with the relationship between the local and the exotic and between the present and the past. The final distribution of the bluestones in the monument at Stonehenge encapsulated the distribution of these different rocks *across their original source area,* with the pieces of spotted dolerite towards its centre and a more scattered distribution of other rock types. In that sense it recreated the distinctive landscape found in south-west Wales in the centre of another, entirely artificial world. That is the material out of which origin myths are formed. The histories of the stones themselves may have encapsulated a narrative that was crucial to the identity of the builders.

These were some of the elements in a perception of the world that was unique in many ways and entirely typical in others. The sheer scale on which these stones were moved and brought together has no precedent in the British Isles, but evidence for the process itself is widespread. It extends from the 'pieces of places' represented by portable artefacts to the transported landscapes that form some of the greatest field monuments. On one level they are at opposite ends of a continuum that extends from artefacts to natural raw materials. On another, they form part of a more basic process that has still to find its place in studies of the ancient world.

Chapter 7

The origin of spaces

Monuments and the natural topography

What does the creation of monuments do to the places where they are built? This chapter is a discussion of the relationship between these structures and natural land forms. It returns to the caves and mountain tops of Crete that played such an important role in the work of Sir Arthur Evans, showing how these features of the terrain were used in the prehistoric period and how they were transformed. This analysis has lessons for work in other areas, and the discussion extends to the early development of monumental architecture in the British Isles. At times, the form and setting of such monuments encapsulate the features of the surrounding landscape and the practices that took place there. The argument is illustrated by the megaliths and decorated caves found in parts of Iberia.

Rude animal shapes

When Arthur Evans came to Crete, Aegean archaeology had reached a turning point. It was changing from a literary and philological pursuit into a discipline whose evidence was collected in the field. From the Renaissance, scholars had used written sources to try to document the places that played a role in the religious life of the ancient world. Among these were the open-air sanctuaries that were associated with particular divinities. Although some of these locations contained ruins, as often as not they were entirely unaltered features of the landscape such as caves and mountain peaks. Some of them had long been known as a source of artefacts, but there was little evidence on which to base a more detailed interpretation.

In some respects, Evans adopted a traditional approach to the evidence. His knowledge of the artefacts led him to suggest that there had been a cult of sacred trees. This argument was based on the study of iconography. He analysed the scenes depicted on some gold rings, which show a tree surrounded by an enclosure wall. The wall itself could be decorated and might be surmounted by horns. Occasionally, the trees are near to a temple building or are shown together with what are interpreted as gods (Figure 28; Evans 1901). Evans's arguments were influenced by the beliefs of living communities in the east Mediterranean and owed very little to the discipline of field archaeology. Although enclosures of

Figure 28 Depiction of an enclosure containing a Minoan
sacred tree
Source: Evans 1901

suitable proportions could be identified on the ground, in most respects his work
followed the conventions of art history.

In other cases, his approach was highly original. He investigated two kinds of
site that are relevant here: the sacred caves of Minoan Crete and the peak sanctuaries. He purchased artefacts from these places and undertook his own fieldwork.
In 1896, he carried out a limited excavation in the cave of Psychro, a site that was
supposedly associated with the infant Zeus. He also surveyed the surface remains
of some of the peak sanctuaries, a class of monument that his research helped to
define. It was only after 1900, when he had already started work at Knossos, that
these places were excavated for the first time (Brown 1993: 37–85).

We must start with the caves, for these would have recalled some of the features
of the sacrificial site that Evans had already investigated in Finland. There are
many natural caves in Crete – the number has been estimated at about 2,000 –
but only a few of these seem to have been selected as cult places. The exact
number is uncertain but probably falls between about twelve (the lowest estimate)
and thirty-six (the highest). The evidence can be difficult to assess (Rutkowski
1986: Chapter 5; Rutkowski and Nowicki 1996; Tyree 1974). Some of the caves
may have been inhabited, but there are few ways to distinguish between a domestic assemblage from these sites and simple offerings of ceramics. The caves may
also have been burial places, but again the evidence is ambiguous. Even when

older material has been found there, it is not clear whether the caves formed part of a sacred landscape before the Minoan period.

There is a further complication for, as happened with the peak sanctuaries, there is little information on the distributions of the different kinds of artefacts or on the sequence in which they were introduced to these sites. One of the most extensive investigations took place at the Psychro Cave and followed a smaller project carried out by Evans himself (Figure 29). The work was not undertaken according to methods that would find favour today: the entrance to the cave was cleared using dynamite, and the exposed deposits were searched by the local people for antiquities. As the excavator reported:

> In the hope of the reward, which I gave for the better objects, and in the excitement of so curious a search, which, in their earlier illicit digging, it had not occurred to them to attempt, the villagers, both men and women, worked with frantic energy, clinging singly to the pillars above the subterranean lake, or grouping half a dozen flaring lights over a productive patch of mud at the water's edge. It was a grotesque sight, without precedent in an archaeologist's experience.
>
> (Hogarth 1900: 100–1)

Figure 29 Plan of the Psychro Cave, Crete, at the time of its excavation
Source: A simplified version of the survey published in Hogarth 1900

Amidst such scenes of chaos, it is remarkable that anything useful was recorded, but in fact there is a little evidence of how these sites were used (Boardman 1961; Watrous 1996). A particular feature of some, but not all, of the cave sanctuaries is the special significance attached to stalagmites and stalactites. Like the Saami *siejddes*, these occurred in extraordinary shapes that resembled the forms of living creatures. They were often selected for special attention. Artefacts might be deposited among these features, or their natural forms could be modified to enhance their resemblance to humans and animals. Some of them were obviously rubbed smooth by the visitors to the caves, whilst fragments of others could even be detached and taken away.

These stalagmites and stalactites result from the presence of water in the caves. Underground water was of special significance. It may have possessed medicinal properties, but it was mainly important because of its unusual origin. It was in the subterranean lake inside the Psychro Cave that a major group of artefacts was found: seal stones, bronze pins, knives, rings and figurines. In one case, such a pool seems to have marked the farthest point at which such offerings were permitted, so that the rear of the cave did not contain any archaeological material. There could also be deposits of weapons in these sites: swords, daggers and the distinctive double axes. Some might be found in water or in clefts in the floors or walls, whilst others could be placed among the natural concretions associated with these places (Rutkowski 1986: Chapter 4; Tyree 1974). There were also more mundane deposits, including slaughtered livestock, cereals and models of domesticated animals.

Several of the caves assumed a monumental aspect during their period of use, although this is less obvious than it is with peak sanctuaries (Rutkowski 1986: Chapter 4; Rutkowski and Nowicki 1996). Artificial spaces could be created in front of the cave mouths where large congregations could gather, and in at least one instance a building, possibly a temple, was constructed there. Altars could be erected in the interior, although natural features were often used instead. Stone walls might also be built to enclose the holiest parts of the cave. Two of these places were decorated with rock art. Its date is difficult to establish, but on one site the images have been attributed to the Minoan period and depict humans, wild animals, birds and fish. In another instance, 'concretions on the wall appear by torch light to spring forth like monsters, and piles of rubble have been arranged into rude animal shapes' (Burkert 1985: 24).

Peak sanctuaries

In some ways, the cave sites contrast with the peak sanctuaries that Evans was investigating at the same time. Although the term may seem self-explanatory, these places share a number of quite specific features (Nowicki 1994; Peatfield 1992; Rutkowski 1986: Chapter 5). At present, there appear to be only twenty-five of these sites in Crete, distributed in three concentrations across the central and eastern parts of the island. The term 'peak sanctuary' is something of a misnomer, as it suggests that they were located on the highest available land. In fact, they are sometimes offset from the mountain top to command an extensive view over the lower ground. They may have been sited so that they could be seen to greatest advantage from below. The peak sanctuaries were intervisible (Peatfield 1996). They were sometimes close to the Minoan palaces and towns, but they also occur in 'rural' areas. Field survey around one of these sites suggests that the mountains lay beyond the limits of the settled landscape.

All these criteria concern the appropriate position for a peak sanctuary, but they do not specify how it should be marked on the ground or what kinds of material should be found there. In each case, there is considerable variation. The extent of the peak sanctuaries is normally determined by the topography of the site, so that it was initially defined in relation to entirely natural boundaries such as outcrops. The sites may include natural terraces, fissures or spectacular rock formations, and one of the largest of this group, at Jouktas, includes a rock fissure within its area (Karelsou 1981). Although many of the sites were enclosed by walls, they do not seem to have been an original feature of these places; nor do the stone buildings whose remains are found there.

Like the sacred caves, these sanctuaries are associated with a variety of different offerings. There seems to be a difference between the contents of the rural peak sanctuaries, like Atsiphades Korakias, and those that are apparently associated with palaces (Peatfield 1992). The rural sanctuaries contain varying amounts of pottery, including models of livestock, and votives that may be connected with human and animal fertility. They also include large numbers of unworked pebbles, which had been introduced from the surrounding lowlands (Nowicki 1994) – a feature curiously reminiscent of the situation at Newgrange and Knowth, described in Chapter 6. The votive deposits may have restricted distributions within the peak sanctuaries, which could have focused on sacred stones or other images, or on natural features of the topography such as clefts in the rock. At Atsiphades Korakias, rather different groups of offerings were associated with each of the terraces on the site (Peatfield 1992).

The sanctuaries located nearer to the Minoan palaces contained a more varied assemblage, and the human and animal figures that are found there are often of higher quality. In contrast to the finds from the sacred caves, offerings of metalwork are very uncommon here, but, like those sites, the major sanctuaries seem to have been associated with large quantities of burnt material, perhaps suggesting that they were used for sacrifice. If so, such evidence seems to be absent from the one extensively excavated example in the countryside (Peatfield 1992).

Unlike the sacred caves, peak sanctuaries are often associated with monumental architecture, although this is not a feature of all the sites. Where it does occur, the structures are much more impressive than those associated with the caves. On the other hand, this was a secondary development in the history of these places, and it seems as if their embellishment with terraces, walls and buildings did not happen until palaces were being built nearby. Thereafter, the history of both types of location often runs in parallel, with the monuments at the peak sanctuary clearly

visible from those on the lower ground. There is disagreement over the significance of this relationship – did the sacred sites come under political control at this
time, and did their history extend beyond the lifespan of the palaces? – but the
sequence itself is quite well documented (Peatfield 1996). It suggests that a variety
of impressive natural places were employed as sacred sites for some time before
monuments were erected in those locations.

What was the nature of the buildings at peak sanctuaries? The limits of some
of these sites were bounded by a wall, although natural rock outcrops were sufficient in some cases. The enclosure wall at the large sanctuary of Jouktas was 3 m
(10 ft) thick, and when it was first described parts of it were 5 m (16 ft) high
(Rutkowski 1986: 75–6). Indeed, it was so impressive that the site has sometimes
been interpreted as a kind of hill fort. Inside the sacred enclosure there could be
stone buildings, although their ground plan is not consistent from one site to
another. At Jouktas, it is likely that the sanctuary comprised a single range of
structures bounding a formal terrace that extended back as far as the edge of a
cliff (Figure 30). The main feature of that terrace was a rock fissure, which
contained a number of offerings. In this case, it seems as if the sacred area was
screened off on three sides.

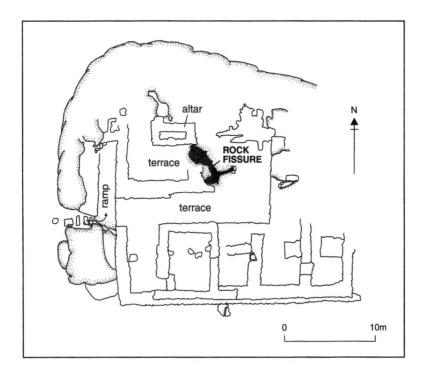

Figure 30 Outline plan of the excavated peak sanctuary at Jouktas, Crete
Source: Information from Karelsou 1981

Jouktas is known in more detail than most of the peak sanctuaries in Crete, but some features do survive. Their basic layout is described by Rutkowski:

> [They] differed from one another in plan. Some . . . had powerful walls, and either the sacred area was built up with terraces, a sacred screen, an altar and a sacred building . . . or terraces formed an open, more or less level space, near which was a sanctuary with several rooms . . . or a small shrine. . . . It can . . . be taken as certain that the detached shrines and temples situated . . . in the peak sanctuaries sometimes consisted of three parts; these buildings had a higher middle part, and a lower part on either side; there was also an entrance (or even more than one) . . . . Especially in the most important shrines, [the] facades were richly decorated with symbols . . . . Religious dances, processions and other ceremonies took place in front of the facade of the shrine. Yet this was not always so, for the shrine was not the most important element of the temenos: the altar was far more important as that was the only object indispensable for cult purposes.
>
> (Rutkowski 1986: 82)

Surviving models suggest that these buildings were often quite elaborate. They were characterised by decorative stonework and could be crowned by 'horns of consecration'. The screens and other structures provided an important focus for votive deposits. At Jouktas, there were numerous objects, including a hoard of double axes found in a pit. There were also clay figures and offering tables (Karelsou 1981).

Although the evidence from these sites is often fragmentary, the most important point is to recognise that all these structures date from the same period as the Minoan palaces (Peatfield 1996). They do not belong to the earliest use of the peak sanctuaries, which were originally organised around the features of the natural topography. In that respect they had more in common with the sacred caves than is sometimes supposed. Whatever the political context of their transformation, that process changed the entire configuration of these sites. There are lessons to be learnt from this example.

Changing places

Any discussion of such changes must proceed with caution, and there is an important qualification to make at the outset. So far, this account has proceeded as if there was always an obvious distinction between monuments and 'natural' places. To some extent that may be a product of our own knowledge and experience. It was not until the seventeenth century AD at the earliest that scholars learnt how to distinguish between artificial constructions and geological features of the landscape. Before that time, there were few criteria for telling them apart, and for two centuries afterwards the uncertainty seems to have persisted. Thus as recently as the nineteenth century there was a spirited campaign to save a megalithic monument in south-west England from destruction, when we would now consider this to have been a granite tor (Evans 1994). In the same region, there is a significant overlap between the forms of the local megaliths and those taken by similar outcrops. This can be interpreted in several different ways (Bradley 1998c). Prehistoric people could have imitated these impressive and durable features of the landscape in their own constructions, in which case they may have sought to give their monuments an impression of age and permanence. Alternatively, lacking a knowledge of field geology, they may have construed these features as the remains of older tombs that had been built in a familiar style of architecture. Since monuments of appropriate form are found well beyond the limits of the granite, this seems just as likely. That may be why megaliths were built within sight of the tors that resembled them so closely, and why some of those distinctive outcrops were incorporated into a series of stone-walled enclosures during the Neolithic period. This is not a unique instance, and it may well be that for the prehistoric inhabitants of Crete, the stone outcrops that characterise the peak sanctuaries might have been thought of as artificial constructions: the work of ancestors or the gods. The natural terraces found on some of these sites could have been conceived as human works, and the same might apply to the strange images formed by the stalagmites and stalactites inside the sacred caves. The history of human constructions might have receded into myth.

Having faced this difficulty, we must address a still more basic question: *what do monuments do to the places where they are built?* This deceptively simple question has many answers.

The first development is perhaps the most basic of all. The construction of monuments in places with an established significance transforms the entire way in which these locations are experienced. The building of walls and terraces at the peak sanctuaries changed the character of these places. Locations that had been readily accessible became more difficult to visit. Parts of the site that had dominated its natural topography could be screened off from view. Where the natural terrain had imposed few constraints on visitors, the presence of walls and terraces influenced – or even directed – the movements of people around the sanctuaries. Particular parts of these sites had to be approached in a prescribed order, and one effect of reconstructing these places was to restrict the numbers of people having access to any one point at the same time. Indeed, the walls built inside the sacred caves may have made the holiest locations virtually inaccessible. Thus the architecture of the cult centres could be used to structure the experiences of the visitors and to determine the extent of their participation in the rituals that were conducted there. The level areas created outside the sacred caves might have accommodated more people who would not have been able to enter the chamber themselves. In the same way, the creation of formal terraces at the peak sanctuaries might have formalised the distinction between those who could visit the shrines or approach the altars and the people who were simply spectators. The new constructions reduced the options of those who made use of the sanctuaries, and in doing so they would have changed the ways in which these sacred spaces were used.

The same is true of other monuments in prehistoric Europe. For example, the Neolithic enclosure at Windmill Hill in Wessex was built on a site that already included a series of pit deposits containing non-local artefacts and at least one human burial (Smith 1965: 22–8; Whittle 1990). It seems possible that at this point it was the hill itself that was significant. The building of the enclosure imposed a formal pattern on what had hitherto been an open space, albeit one set apart from the pattern of settlement. Now the hill was defined by three successive circuits of ditches, breached by numerous entrances converging on the centre. Each of the entrances faced in a different direction, suggesting the passage of people to and from the surrounding area. As they crossed these thresholds, they left appropriate offerings (Whittle and Pollard 1998). At the same time, the creation of these earthworks meant that space was increasingly graded (Figure 31). There were two separate zones in between the ditches and a further, unstructured area outside. Each of

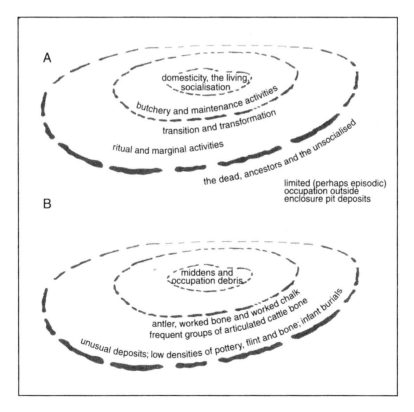

Figure 31 Plan of the Neolithic enclosure at Windmill Hill, Wiltshire, England, summarising the interpretation proposed in Whittle and Pollard 1998

these zones may have had different associations, just as each successive boundary to the enclosure was associated with different kinds of material. Whittle and Pollard (1998) suggest that the deepest space was associated with domesticity and the living, and the outer zone with ritual. The deposits in the ditches reflect some of these distinctions. Those in the inner ditch include occupation debris. The middle ditch contains groups of articulated cattle bone as well as evidence for the production of artefacts, whilst the outer ditch includes human remains and the burials of children.

The interpretation of these patterns matters rather less than the character of that transformation, for once again the creation of a monument in what was already a special place altered the ways in which it could be used. Instead of an open hill top, people were faced with a complex subdivision of space in which the appropriate places for particular activities – and for particular deposits – were increasingly circumscribed. This is not to suggest the imposition of centralised authority on the site, for it may still have met the needs of a dispersed population, but now their traditional activities were attended by a far greater formality. Practices that had been associated with different parts of the landscape – feasting, artefact production, the commemoration of the dead – may have been brought together, until the enclosure contained all the elements found in the wider world.

A second way in which the creation of monuments changes the character of places is through the scale on which they are built. This has two distinct aspects. First, it makes particular places much more visible. For example, the architecture of the Cretan peak sanctuaries was clearly intended to be seen from the palaces on the lower ground. The sacred sites were also meant to be seen from one another (Peatfield 1996). At the same time, the recreation of special places through building projects involves a new kind of participation and a new level of commitment. However the work of building these structures was organised, they made demands on human labour that could have been met only by the creation of considerable work forces. These need not have been employed continuously over long periods, but the very fact that so many people were drawn into the construction of these monuments meant that they entered into a closer relationship with such places. The sanctuaries assumed a more powerful role in their daily lives, just as their architecture came to dominate the landscapes round about them.

Again, that proposition can be illustrated by some of the monuments of the Avebury area. Long after the earthworks of Windmill Hill fell into disrepair, the site seems to have retained its local importance and deposits of artefacts continued to be placed in the tops of its ditches. Similar activities went on in other areas, but the geographical focus of activity gradually changed, so that lowland basins or other places with an all-round view assumed a greater significance. Like Colin Richards, I have argued that 'circular' landscapes of this kind became the focus for a series of circular monuments built during the later Neolithic period (Richards 1996b; Bradley 1998a: Chapter 8), but that argument does not account for the very different scales on which they were constructed. For example, Overton Hill, the source of the Avebury Avenue, was already associated with deposits of artefacts before the earliest monument was built there (Smith and Simpson 1964: 82 and 1966: 151). This was a timber circle, the Sanctuary, located on a prominent spur with a view over part of the Kennet Valley (Figure 32). The circle was not enclosed by any earthwork but eventually it seems as if the wooden posts were replaced by two concentric rings of monoliths (Pollard 1992). On a nearby spur is a very different monument, Silbury Hill. In contrast to the Sanctuary, this is a structure of unique proportions, which seems to have been built in stages at roughly the same time as Avebury itself (Whittle 1997: 5–49). It is, quite literally, an artificial hill, and on its summit there is a level platform. Although the excavated evidence is not clear-cut, the first structure on this site may have been a ring of stakes enclosing exactly the same area as the timber circle at the Sanctuary. The interior of this setting was filled with turves, brought specially to the site, and then the entire structure was buried beneath a mound more than 30 m (98 ft) in diameter and over 5 m (16ft) high. This earthwork was subsequently enlarged until the entire construction rose to a height of no less than 37 m (121 ft). The platform on its summit was the same size as the original mound and was located vertically above it. More important, it was virtually the same size and shape as a Late Neolithic palisaded enclosure on the valley floor nearby. This contained another timber circle (Whittle 1997: 76–82). The platform on top of Silbury Hill was larger than the post setting at the Sanctuary and rather smaller than the stone circle that took its place. We do not know whether that platform was occupied by anything similar, but it was another circular enclosure cut off from its surroundings by an artificial feature of the landscape. In this case, its scale is all-important. The crest of the great mound would have been difficult to reach and could never have held many people, yet it was a monument that involved the participation of a considerable work force and one that must have been recognisable from much of the surrounding area.

The third characteristic of monumental architecture is that it can invest significant natural places with additional layers of symbolism. This is particularly obvious in the case of the peak sanctuaries, where the walls of the structures were elaborately decorated and were crowned by 'horns of consecration'. The same would apply to the shrines erected on these sites and also to the altars that played such an important role in ritual. These symbolic structures could have been of two main kinds. First, there was the degree of embellishment that is possible with monumental architecture. The surfaces of the walls were elaborately treated and some of them may have been painted. Certain of the buildings included pillars, and even the natural features inside a few of the caves seem to have been affected, by modifying the natural concretions or even by the creation of rock art. At the same time, the structural framework that became such a feature of the peak sanctuaries may have made it possible to create quite specific relationships between particular parts of these buildings and particular kinds of offering. There is evidence for the careful organisation of such material inside the caves and rural peak sanctuaries. The creation of formal architecture in these places may have made these patterns more explicit and could even have imbued them with a more

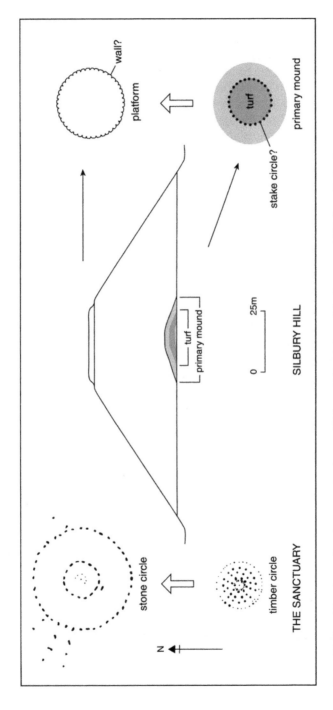

Figure 32 Possible relationships between the design of Silbury Hill and that of the Sanctuary, Wiltshire, England

specific significance. This would be particularly true if the erection of these structures meant that participants in the rituals would need to move around these spaces in a prescribed order. I shall return to this observation in Chapter 8.

We can see rather similar principles at work in Cornwall, where I have already commented on the striking resemblance between the natural granite formations and the appearance of local megalithic tombs. The enclosed site at Carn Brea provides an excellent example of these processes (Mercer 1981). On one level it is a prominent, even dramatic, hill top, whose distinctive appearance was enhanced by the creation of several circuits of ditches, ramparts and walls. Inside the enclosures there is evidence of settlement, and excavation has defined the positions of several houses. Beyond the enclosures, on the lower slopes of the hill, there seems to have been cultivated land, and here we find a series of clearance cairns. At the same time, there is little doubt that the enclosure walls were intended to protect the interior, as the large number of arrowheads recovered from the site suggest that it had come under attack. Enclosures with some of the same characteristics are known elsewhere in south-west England and further to the north along the coastline of the Irish Sea (Mercer 1981: 193–5).

That is a selective account of Carn Brea, and none of these points is at all controversial, but there are elements that suggest another level of significance. The various stone and earthwork circuits on the site have been interpreted as successive enclosures, one replacing another, but they could equally well represent the increasing subdivision of the interior. The process may also refer to the grading of space. That would certainly explain why the innermost enclosure on Carn Brea encloses a massive rock outcrop and has little room for any buildings. At the same time, the excavator has observed how the walls of the enclosures run from one rock outcrop to another (Mercer 1981: 62–3). This enhances their appearance but hardly adds to the practicality of the overall design. On the other hand, some of these outcrops – especially those associated with the innermost enclosure – bear a striking resemblance to the megalithic tombs found in the same area (Figure 33; Bradley 1998c). Similar features are associated with the defensive circuits of other enclosures in the region, and these sites may be of similar date.

The explicit attention paid to the rock formations at Carn Brea may have yet another meaning, for the area close to the site was one of the major sources of Neolithic axes in Britain, and a large number of them have been found in the enclosure itself. Many more are known in areas further to the east, including a number of examples from Windmill Hill. Again, the attention paid to these particular axes may owe something to the distinctive character of the region in which they were produced. Although those axes were not made on Carn Brea itself, they may have been distributed through the site, so that the exotic material from which they were made could have been associated with the extraordinary rock formations on the hill top (Mercer 1981: 153–60). The important point is that the monumental architecture of Carn Brea could make so many different references. It enclosed and protected a domestic settlement, but it also monumentalised a series of granite tors that bore a strong resemblance to megalithic tombs.

Figure 33 A natural rock formation, resembling a megalithic tomb, built into the wall of the Neolithic enclosure at Carn Brea, Cornwall, south-west England

Moreover, Carn Brea was associated with the production and distribution of stone axes, whose distinctive properties were recognised in areas far away from the site. These are some of the ways in which the building of monuments can add new meanings to natural places.

The monument as the landscape

I conclude Part 2 with an example from the archaeology of northern Iberia that brings a number of these different themes together.

As we saw in Chapter 5, this area is characterised by two distinctive traditions of rock art. In northern Portugal and neighbouring parts of Spain, it seems that schematic art may have played a specialised role. It was located in remote parts of the landscape, in places that were set apart from the wider pattern of settlement. These included cliffs, caves and rock shelters that could never have held many people. The images found there may owe a little to the visions seen in altered states of consciousness, and the most elaborate painted panels can sometimes be found in the least accessible locations. Within this region, schematic art is often associated with impressive features of the landscape and with places that are dangerous and remote. For all these reasons, the decorated sites are often interpreted as sanctuaries.

In contrast to schematic art, Galician rock art was strongly linked to the domestic domain. Although the distributions of these two traditions complement one another, an element that is common to both of them is the presence of cup marks. As these are among the simplest motifs, the overlap is not surprising. In northern Portugal, however, the distribution of cup-marked rocks is strikingly different from that of more complex designs. For the most part, they are discovered in low-lying positions that would have been well suited to year-round settlement (Sanches *et al.* 1998). Cup marks are difficult to date, but at least some of these examples should be contemporary with the schematic paintings and carvings. If that is true, then it suggests a very basic division in the prehistoric landscape. Cup marks are found in the domestic world, where they may occupy quite inconspicuous places, whilst schematic art is beyond its limits and is associated with altogether more specialised locations.

That same distinction is enshrined in the decoration of megalithic tombs in northern Iberia. In Galicia, there is little overlap between tomb art and the motifs found in the open air, yet the outer limits of several important cemeteries are marked by a system of cup-marked rocks (Villoch 1995). The structure of the decorated tombs is interesting too, for the motifs that overlap most clearly with schematic art are generally found in the deepest spaces inside these monuments (Jorge 1998). This relationship became even more apparent with the recent discovery near Badajoz of cave paintings that depict some of the objects which are usually associated with these structures (Collado *et al.* 1997). Cup marks have a wider distribution in the megalithic tombs, extending towards the entrance and to the surface of the capstone (Bueno and Balbín 1992: 529). Again, their chronology is by no means clear, but the spatial relationship between these two groups of motifs does seem to mirror their distribution across the area as a whole. This evidence suggests that in one sense the organisation of the tomb art summarised the attributes of the surrounding area. In that way, the structure of these monuments has features in common with the organisation of the wider landscape.

There is one site that brings all these different elements together. This is El Pedroso in Castille (Esparza 1977). The site is situated on the Spanish/Portuguese border and is currently being investigated by Germán Delibes, Ramón Fábregas and the writer. El Pedroso is a distinctive granite hill, set apart from its surrounding by its characteristic geology, which has resulted in the creation of a series of striking landforms. The summit of the hill is enclosed by a massive wall dating from the Copper Age. In places, this follows the configuration of the natural outcrops. Inside the hill fort, there is a group of circular houses and what was probably a tower. Within the occupied area, there was also an arrowhead workshop.

On the flank of the same hill, but invisible from the fort itself, there is a rock formation that is very similar in appearance to the granite tors of south-west England. This can be identified from some distance away. There are natural fissures in the granite that have resulted in the formation of a cave (Figure 34). It has two distinct chambers, separated from one another by a narrow opening. Each is associated with panels of rock carvings. Those located in the outer part of

Figure 34 **The setting of the decorated cave at El Pedroso, Zamora, northern Spain**

the cave include many cup marks, whilst the deepest spaces – those in the second chamber – are characterised by a much more varied series of images, including human figures, which can be identified as schematic art. The two styles are, of course, those found in different areas of the wider landscape, but inside the cave at El Pedroso their distributions do not overlap. The cup marks, whose counterparts are found in fertile lowland areas, are in the most accessible part of the site. The other images are farthest from the entrance, and their counterparts are in more remote areas of the landscape. The cave contains Copper and Bronze Age pottery and other artefacts, and just outside it field-work in 1998 revealed the remains of two massive terraces bounded by dry-stone walls. El Pedroso is clearly another natural location whose use has been formalised by monumental architecture.

On one level, this site could be compared with the simpler cult places of Crete, for it makes use of some of the same kinds of feature. It shows a similar mixture of natural and artificial elements: a cave, two terraces and, in this case, several panels of rock art. But more local comparisons can be equally revealing. The first use of the cave 'sanctuary' is contemporary with the defences on the hill top, and it also exhibits the same organisation of space as a megalithic tomb, with its forecourt, entrance passage and chamber. That connection is emphasised by the distribution of the rock carvings. Yet even that comparison is insufficient, for, more than that, the layout of the petroglyphs at El Pedroso recalls the distribution of carved motifs on natural surfaces across the landscape as a whole. In that way, the cave sanctuary might also have acted as a model of the surrounding area.

The cave at El Pedroso, and probably the terraces, may have been associated with specialised deposits. Some of these extend to the foot of the decorated surfaces. Fine arrowheads were being made inside the hill fort, and the entire outcrop was monumentalised by the building of stone walls. This distinctive group of features brings together all the elements discussed in Part 2 of this book. They illustrate very well what is meant by an archaeology of natural places, but in doing so they introduce a more important issue. In this example, I have tried to relate these features to the configuration of an entire landscape. How far is this possible in other areas? Part 3 provides more extended case studies that investigate this problem.

Part 3

Interpretations

Some eyes condemn the earth they gaze upon:
Some wait patiently till they know far more
Than earth can tell them. . . .

'Some eyes condemn', Thomas 1920

Chapter 8

The history of the world

A case study from Neolithic Britain

The first case study is concerned with British prehistory, and focuses on the way in which artefacts that had been associated with quite specific types of places were brought together through the creation of monuments. The deposits that are found there have often been investigated as an end in themselves, yet a closer analysis of these finds shows that they must have been made and viewed in a certain sequence. In that respect, they are rather like a narrative. Such deposits may have formed in the course of relating origin myths, so that the experience of moving around such places recreated the processes by which the world was made.

Part 3 of this book offers a sequence of case studies, or 'Interpretations' as I prefer to call them. The first concerns the later Neolithic period in Britain, the second considers the Bronze Age landscape of southern Scandinavia, whilst the third covers an altogether larger area and a longer period of time. It extends into the Iron Age and discusses the changing role of natural places in the archaeology of northern and western Europe. The focus of these studies changes too. The present chapter is concerned with production sites, structured deposition and the evidence of monuments. Chapter 9 is primarily concerned with the interpretation of rock art and its relationship to burial mounds, whilst Chapter 10 discusses the importance of votive deposits in European archaeology, and the ways in which their distribution and significance varied over time. Each, then, is concerned with the ways in which the separate elements considered in Part 2 were brought together in the ancient landscape.

The structure of structured deposits

The first study takes structured deposition as its point of departure. This topic became a major focus of research in Neolithic studies during the 1980s, and the success of this approach has influenced scholars working on other periods (Hill 1995: Chapter 10; Thomas 1991: Chapter 4). In recent years, it has assumed a growing significance in accounts of later prehistory.

What is structured deposition and how has it been studied? Put very simply, this term describes the ways in which material culture is organised on its deposition in the ground. It is concerned with the manner in which the contents of pits, ditches and post holes seem to have been structured in the past and can be identified through recurrent patterns of association and exclusion. The same principle applies to material that was never buried but may have been placed in other kinds of location, such as rivers and lakes (Bradley 1990a: Chapter 1; Thomas 1991: Chapter 4).

We can study this phenomenon at many different levels, from the organisation of the different deposits to their position in the landscape. The most important point is that restricted groups of artefacts, human remains and animal bones are frequently found together in apparent isolation. Accounts of these deposits show that this material had not been assembled by chance and that it had been arranged with some formality. Although most attention has been paid to the contents of pits and ditches, such finds have an altogether wider distribution. Rather than beginning this discussion with the finds from earthwork monuments, it may be better to start with the deposits found in natural places.

Structured deposits have many different aspects. They can contain different assemblages of material, they can be found in different kinds of locations from one another, and the objects contained within them may have had very different histories. It is difficult to disentangle all these separate elements, and this account deals with just some of the possibilities.

Let us start with the question of space. Different locations often produce their own distinctive assemblages. Julian Thomas makes this point when he discusses the groups of material associated with the main ceramic styles of the later Neolithic period in Britain: Peterborough Ware and Grooved Ware (1996: 164–8). Although their chronologies may overlap to a limited extent, there is little to indicate that one tradition was the direct successor of the other. Rather, each style was associated with quite different kinds of deposit:

> The pre-existing character of a place demanded the use of a specific set of items. Two context types where this seems to be indicated are caves and wet places, including rivers and bogs. In the case of caves, there is a particularly strong association between human bones and Peterborough Ware. . . . In a similar way, rivers, bogs and other wet places received a distinctive set of deposits in the later Neolithic. Here again, Peterborough Ware vessels are encountered, but whole and unbroken, while Grooved Ware is totally absent. . . . Axes, too, seem to have been introduced into rivers in large numbers and in unbroken condition. . . . The . . . Thames has also produced a large number of . . . mace heads.
>
> (1994: 177)

He observes that particular kinds of material may be found together in contexts where other objects are largely absent (Figure 35). For example, seashells, fossils, carved chalk objects and oblique transverse arrowheads all occur together with

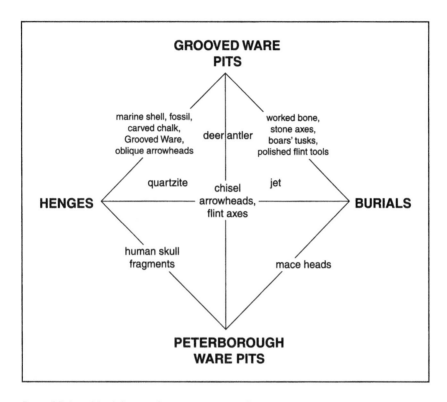

Figure 35 Late Neolithic artefact associations in Britain
Source: Julian Thomas 1996

Grooved Ware, but this assemblage hardly overlaps with another set of associ-ations consisting of worked bone, stone axes, boars' tusks and artefacts of polished flint. In the same way, chisel arrowheads can be found with flint axes, but neither is regularly associated with these other kinds of material. Even if some of these artefacts were employed on the same occasions, they were carefully separated from one another when their use was over.

Another important point has been made by Andrew Jones (1998) in his recent analysis of the animal remains associated with chambered cairns in Orkney: the organisation of some of these deposits can reflect quite basic perceptions of the landscapes in which they were made. The assemblages that he studied are of two different kinds. The first pre-date the construction of the tombs, and seem to indicate that particular places already played a special role in the landscape. The composition of these 'foundation deposits' seems to be determined by their pos-ition in the terrain. The same depositional patterns may have continued after the tombs were built.

Thus the remains of sea eagles were deposited in tombs on the coast or on cliffs, whilst the bones of other birds are more widely distributed. Finds of domesticated animals predominated on the lower ground in areas suitable for settlement, whilst deposits of red deer bones were found on higher land, which is their typical habitat. 'Animals [were] being used actively as a medium by which people [were] relating themselves to the landscape' (Jones 1998: 315). Jones goes on to argue that the same distinctions were important in the treatment of the human dead. The tombs in low-lying positions towards the heart of the domestic world contained complete skeletons. Those towards its limits on the higher ground included disarticulated remains, whilst the monuments in the uplands, which could also be associated with finds of red deer, generally contained human skulls. Thus different places were marked by different kinds of offering, and this scheme extended to the treatment of the dead in the chambered tombs. Whole bodies were associated with the settled land and isolated skulls with the areas that lay outside it.

In this last example, the different deposits evoke the special character of the places where they are found: thus sea eagles are associated with the coastline, whilst red deer are associated with the hills. There are other deposits whose distinctive contents evoke links with distant areas.

This is particularly true of another kind of material: stone axes. Chapter 6 explained how one of the most obvious characteristics of the British and Irish Neolithic is the long distances over which axe heads seem to have been moved and the distinctive contexts in which some of them have been found. For instance, a recent study of Irish stone axes suggests that many more examples have been found in natural locations than occur at archaeological sites. Such 'sites' account for 167 of these artefacts, and another 68 come from monuments or related features. These apparently high figures are put in perspective by over 900 axes from river beds and nearly 250 from bogs (Cooney and Mandal 1998: 34–8). The stone axes found in Ireland include a small number of Cumbrian artefacts transported across the water and what may be jadeite axes whose origins were in the foothills of the Alps. Axes were exported as well, and nearly 200 porcellanite axes were identified to be from Ulster so that they must have been moved across the Irish Sea.

It is difficult to discuss the character of all the axe heads exchanged during the Neolithic period. Some were in pristine condition and must have been deposited in their original state, whilst others had remained in circulation for some time and showed signs of use, resharpening and repair (Chappell 1987). Their most important characteristic is that they had been ground or polished, for this brings out the distinctive qualities of the raw material and makes it quite easily identifiable, even at some distance from the source. Although this kind of treatment does improve the mechanical performance of these tools, the process goes well beyond what was necessary (Bradley and Edmonds 1993: 49). It has less to do with utility than with style.

Cumbrian axes were also moved across the Pennines into eastern England, where their treatment is most revealing. A number of them were deposited with some formality, unlike similar artefacts made out of local stone. It may be that the Lake District axes held a special significance because of the remote and dangerous places where they had been made. The same may well apply to the products of other highland quarries. The clearest evidence of this is a small group of axe heads found along the North Sea coast that had been perforated for use as ornaments. These 'axe pendants' were found only in areas remote from the sources of the raw material, and there is circumstantial evidence that a number of them had been used as tools before this happened (Bradley 1990b).

The question of origins is important in still another way. The 'biographical' approach to the study of artefacts has become a notable feature of recent writing. It is a method that follows the life history of particular objects from the circumstances of their creation through to their final deposition, when their separate identities were extinguished. It may be worth taking this approach a little further. We have seen that axe heads and decorated pottery might be buried in pits, but if specialised objects of this kind can be thought of as carrying their histories with them, then surely that knowledge might have influenced the precise manner in which they were deposited. In a number of quite different cases, it seems as if these objects returned to the elements from which they were formed. That may be one of the most basic processes linking particular kinds of material to the places where they are discovered.

A few examples may make this clear. Later Neolithic deposits in southern England contain a variety of carved chalk objects. Although these could have circulated as widely as any other artefacts, the great majority of them were deposited in pits or shafts excavated into the chalk itself. In the same way, a number of stone axes imported across the Pennines into north-east England seem to have been deposited in rock fissures. Again, it seems as if they needed to be returned to an appropriate medium. A similar observation has been made by Gabriel Cooney in a study of other quarry sites:

> The working of stone on axe production sites is not solely a case of rough-outs being produced – a lot of ... debitage is also created .... It should not be regarded just as waste but as something ... which was culturally important.... If we accept the debitage as a form of deposit ... we should not be surprised that ... there is clear evidence for the deliberate placement back in the ground of material associated with the working of the rock .... *It seems plausible to suggest that the deposition may represent a deliberate offering of material concerned with working stone and other activities back to the earth.*
>
> (Cooney 1998: 114; my emphasis)

Among the examples that he mentions are pits with placed deposits of decorated pottery and stone working tools found at the quarry site on Lambay Island, and similar deposits inside a Neolithic enclosure at Goodland in Ulster, where the positions of some of the features containing flaking debris and other artefacts had been marked by cairns.

A similar process is apparent in north-east England, where high-quality arrowheads and knives were produced in two small workshops inside a large settlement site on the Yorkshire Wolds. It was here that they were flaked and polished using raw material introduced from the coast, yet some of the completed artefacts were deliberately destroyed and deposited in other parts of the same site, where they occur along with axes that had been brought from Cumbria. Durden suggests that these objects were returned to their original source when their useful life was over (1995: 431).

It seems possible that similar considerations applied to pottery and human remains. For some time it has been apparent that Neolithic mortuary rituals involved a complex process. The bodies of specific people were exposed or buried until the flesh was gone and individual bones had lost their articulation. Selected relics might be taken away and could circulate between a whole series of different archaeological contexts. These might include settlement locations, in which case this practice would have something in common with the evidence just described. After a period during which they were treated like portable artefacts, bones belonging to particular individuals were returned to their original source. In this case, that could have been the settlements where those people had lived (Thomas 1991: Chapter 6).

Grooved Ware may have gone through a rather similar history. This is the earliest style of pottery in the British Isles to be tempered with grog: a practice that continued through the Bell Beaker phase until the end of the Early Bronze Age (Cleal 1995). It involves the recycling of broken ceramics in the production of new vessels, and whilst this helps to produce a robust fabric, it does seem curious that it should have been most important during precisely the period in which ceramics themselves played a specialised role. Perhaps this was regarded as an analogous process, so that at the end of their period of use certain vessels were reduced to their original constituents and mixed back into potting clay. That is particularly relevant in the case of Grooved Ware, as there is evidence that decorated vessels had been mended so that they could be used for longer (Cleal 1988). This did not happen with other styles of pottery during this period.

Taken together, these practices emphasise the sheer complexity of the phenomenon that has become known as structured deposition. The placing of material in the ground involved a whole series of references – to the origins of objects, to their history and to the significance of particular places in the landscape – and it involved a series of conventions about which kinds of material might be associated together and which needed to be kept apart. It also merged artefacts with human and animal remains in a way that cut across any stereotyped division between culture and nature. Thus human remains could be passed about the landscape in the same way as portable objects. Each of these deposits might have encapsulated basic ideas about the world. If so, then what would happen when those different groups of material were brought together in the fabric of monuments?

Deposits inside monuments

Some of these patterns had been apparent since the 1970s, but they did not become a major focus of research until they were studied in relation to a number of monuments in southern England. Although pit deposits could be found in the vicinity of these sites, there was more interest in the activities taking place within them. From the beginning, this was concerned with the interpretation of the monuments, which had become a controversial matter. Even the excavator of the great henge at Durrington Walls changed his mind after the results of his field-work were published (Wainwright and Longworth 1971). Having first interpreted the site as a ceremonial centre, he suggested that it might have been a settlement (Wainwright 1975: 67). More recently, he seems to have returned to his original ideas (Wainwright 1989: Chapter 6). That is because the field evidence takes such a distinctive form.

Studies of henge monuments and their associations have focused on two main questions: how were the contents of these sites organised, and what were the processes by which different kinds of material had come into the archaeological record? Behind these concerns was a broader agenda, for the real aim of this work was to investigate the archaeological evidence for ritual activity at henges. The work depended on one basic assumption: if ritual could be characterised by formal patterns of behaviour, might it be possible to investigate the character of these monuments by working out how material items had been deposited within them? This was an idea pursued by Colin Richards and Julian Thomas (1984). If sites like Durrington Walls, Woodhenge and Mount Pleasant contained what could be interpreted as formal deposits, this would surely show that they had been ceremonial centres. Of course, there is a flaw in this reasoning and it is not a position that either of these authors would take today. It is quite clear that ritual permeates every part of social life and that it can take place in a settlement just as it does in a shrine. An archaeological demonstration of that point is provided by work on Iron Age hill forts (Hill 1995).

Structured deposition became an accepted part of Neolithic studies, but at just the time when it commanded most attention prehistorians took another approach to the interpretation of monuments. They began to recreate the experiences of past actors as they used these sites (Thomas 1990 and 1991: Chapter 3). It was a study that emphasised movement and vision. How would people have found their way around those places? What might they have been allowed to see? Was every-one permitted to take part, or were certain people privileged whilst others were excluded? The distribution of deposits was not forgotten entirely, but now it was assimilated into another kind of analysis. It suggested how people had circulated around these structures and it identified some of the places that seemed to be of special significance. In most cases, the discussion ended there.

Perhaps we can bring both these approaches together. To take one specific example, between 1908 and 1913, Harold St George Gray excavated the Neo-lithic henge monument at Maumbury Rings in Dorset. When I published his excavation many years later, I became aware that the contents of this monument were very peculiar indeed (Bradley 1975; Bradley and Thomas 1984). The site consisted of a ring of shafts, dug 10 m (33 ft) or more into the solid chalk. There was an external bank and a single entrance. The overall distribution of material in the filling of the pits was extremely uneven. There were more finds in the right-hand half of the enclosure than there were to the left, and groups of adjacent shafts seem to have been refilled to the same levels simultaneously. As this happened, certain combinations of artefacts and bones were placed within them. There were several distinct episodes of deposition, and it soon became clear that the finds from the lower parts of the pits were of a very different character from those towards the top. For instance, pottery was at the bottom of these shafts, carved chalk objects were mainly in the middle of the filling and so were the skulls of stags. Antler picks had a completely different distribution from pieces of unworked antler, and all the human remains were found towards the surface. The extraordinary nature of this site means that there must have been another dimension to these deposits. Given the sheer depth of the pits – the deepest went nearly 12 m (39 ft) into the chalk – this material was obviously deposited over a period of time, yet the radiocarbon dates from different levels were the same. Not only were particular materials associated with or separated from one another, but they must have been placed in these pits *in a prescribed sequence*. Virtually the same pattern has been identified in a smaller monument of the same kind, at Wyke Down, elsewhere in Dorset (Figure 36). This excavation, by Martin Green, was of much higher quality and here it is possible to suggest how these deposits were organised (Table 5; Barrett *et al.* 1991: 92–106).

The logistics of placing material in the shafts at Wyke Down or Maumbury Rings make these particularly suitable examples to discuss, but in fact rather similar arguments apply to other sites. We can just as easily consider the excavated

Table 5 The pattern of deposition in the henge monument at Wyke Down, Dorset

Primary contexts	Primary and secondary contexts	Secondary contexts
Carved chalk		
Antler picks		
Other antler		
Stoneworking tools		
	Retouched artefacts	
	Cattle	
	Pig	
	Red deer	
		Grooved Ware
		Human cremations
		Human skull
		Sheep/goat

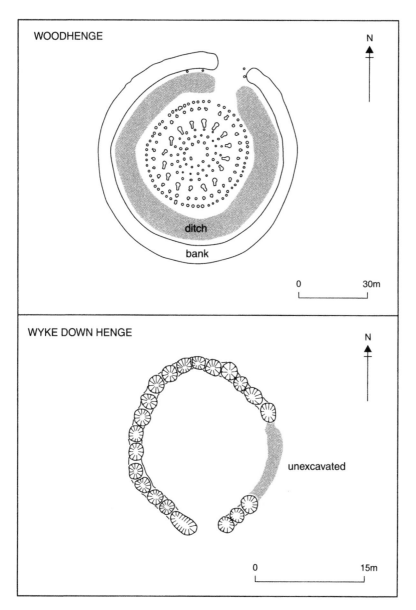

Figure 36 Outline plans of the henge monuments at Woodhenge, Wiltshire, and Wyke Down, Dorset, England

material from Woodhenge (Figure 36), a monument that has been carefully studied by Julian Thomas (1991: 71–3) and by Joshua Pollard (1995). Here there seems to be a gradient in the distribution of the finds. The remains of wild animals were towards the exterior, and so were pig bones, but the remains of domesticated cattle increased in numbers towards the centre. The overall scheme involved other kinds of material, including stone tools, carved chalk objects and human remains. As Table 6 indicates, these deposits were distributed in relation to the concentric organisation of the monument, and the very structure of the building ensured that different groups of material would be encountered in a set order. The position of some of these deposits at the foot of upright posts has even been treated as a clue to the pattern of movement around this monument (Pollard 1995). The same is true of the henges at Mount Pleasant and Durrington Walls, where rather similar evidence has been recognised (Richards and Thomas 1984; Thomas 1996: Chapter 7).

It is here that the finds of decorated pottery have a contribution to make. How was this material organised on its deposition at these sites? Important contrasts can be seen on a variety of scales. At the extensively excavated site of Mount Pleasant, the simplest vessels, some of them undecorated, come from the enclosure ditch, whilst the most complex forms are associated with the timber circle in its interior (Thomas 1996: 197–205). At Durrington Walls, the most elaborately decorated vessels came from the larger of the timber circles excavated on the site. Others were associated with a platform beside its entrance. The vessels found with the other post setting took a simpler form (Richards and Thomas 1984). In the most extensively excavated timber circle (Structure 2) at West Kennet, there is still more subtle patterning, for here undecorated vessels were associated with the entrance to the structure and more elaborate pottery with the back of the monument (Whittle 1997: 117). Again, this could be related to the sequence in which this material was offered or viewed. The simpler vessels were placed in the entrance, and those with the most complex designs were in the deepest space inside the building.

Table 6 The pattern of deposition at Woodhenge, Wiltshire

Exterior/entrance	→	Intermediate	→	Central area
Stone axe Wild cattle bones Wild pig bones Human skulls		Human skull Human cremation Chalk axes Other worked chalk Stone axe fragments		
Human burial — — — — → — — — — →		Domesticated cattle bones increase Domesticated pig bones decrease		Human burial? — — — — → — — — — →

My point is a very simple one. The work of the last few years has shown that the Neolithic monuments of Wessex have a quite specific structure and that this can be understood in terms of the movements of the people who went there. On sites like the timber circles at Woodhenge or Mount Pleasant, their progress seems to have been guided by a series of corridors and screens that provided access to the centre. If people moved about these buildings in a prescribed order, it follows that the deposits placed against the upright posts must have been viewed in sequence. Most likely, they were also *placed there* in a set order. This means that we can not only recognise the *spatial* organisation of different kinds of deposit, we can also identify a *temporal* dimension to this material.

It is worth returning to some of the monuments that have been mentioned already. One way of looking at the evidence from Maumbury Rings is to say that carved chalk objects were deposited at the same time as the skulls of stags, and that human remains could be introduced only at a later stage. At Wyke Down, carved chalk objects, antler and artefacts connected with the working of flint were all deposited before decorated pottery and human bones, and the same approach can be taken to the timber circles of Wessex. At Woodhenge, the bones of wild animals had to be offered (or viewed) before the remains of domesticates, and at Mount Pleasant offerings of pig bone – or more probably of pork – were associated with an earlier stage in the ritual than the offerings of beef. Each of these conventions is clearly documented at a particular site. They are by no means uniform from one monument to another, but they were *expressed in similar ways* across the region as a whole.

Rituals are often a way of telling a story. They may re-enact important narratives concerned with how the world came into being, and sometimes they tell how the human population is related to the past and the supernatural. Those rituals are often orchestrated by the use of powerful symbols. Perhaps the successive deposits found in the Wessex henges may have acted in rather the same way. They illustrated some of the stages in a narrative that was important in the rituals that were conducted there. Each of the deposits described in this chapter could have had wider connotations. The distinction between wild and domestic animals must have been fundamental to Neolithic identity, but the contrast between cattle and pigs could have had just as many implications for the history of the society that made these offerings. Pigs were domesticated from the wild, whilst domesticated cattle had to be introduced from the Continent. Axes are associated with the clearance of the natural forest, which was originally inhabited by red deer. At Woodhenge, there was a sequence leading from the wild to the domestic; at Maumbury Rings it led from the skulls of red deer to those of human beings; and at Wyke Down the sequence extended from carved chalk objects to flint artefacts and then to decorated pottery. Only the latter group was associated with human remains. The details are less important than the general pattern, for it is unwise to insist on a single reading of such a sequence of deposits. It is much more important to establish what kind of phenomenon we are investigating. I suggest that it is a narrative concerned with history, with origins and with the place of people in the world.

At the same time, it may also be a history that involves quite other places, for the forms taken by some of the artefacts evoke connections with more distant locations. This is especially true of the ground stone axes that had been brought from far away. The finds from Wyke Down, for instance, include a complete axe head from Wales and a decorated pottery vessel that is linked to similar material in Orkney (Barrett *et al.* 1991: 96–102). Maumbury Rings included a chalk drum like those known from north-east England (Bradley 1975: 25), and Mount Pleasant contained an Early Bronze Age axe (Wainwright 1979a: Chapter 10). Connections of this kind are even more obvious with the adoption of Bell Beaker pottery, whose distribution extended across large parts of Continental Europe. The sequence of deposits at these sites might evoke distant places as well as distant times.

The best illustration of this point comes from Mount Pleasant, where a monument that was originally associated with Grooved Ware continued in use during the Beaker phase. On one level, little seems to have changed. The main groups of Beaker ceramics were distributed in the same areas as the Neolithic pottery, and in both phases deposits of animal bones seem to have been employed to highlight important differences of space within the area of the monument (Thomas 1996: 208–12).

On the other hand, the Beaker pottery from Mount Pleasant may introduce yet another dimension to the problems of structured deposition. There are two major pottery sequences in the stratified levels on the site (Thomas 1996: 212–22). These are associated with the northern entrance to the main henge enclosure and with the ditch that surrounds the timber circle (Figure 37). The deposits from the northern entrance follow an orderly sequence, leading from Grooved Ware in the Neolithic period to a succession of Early Bronze Age styles: first Beakers, then Food Vessels, then Collared Urns and, finally, Bucket Urns. This is the generally accepted sequence in Wessex, based on the evidence of other excavated sites. In the ditch on Site IV, however, this orderly pattern is upset. The lower levels of the ditch contain earlier Neolithic pottery as well as Grooved Ware, despite the fact that these styles were in use hundreds of years apart. Beaker pottery is found throughout the filling of the ditch, sometimes in association with the very styles that seem to replace it in the entrance to the monument. At first sight, it seems as if this material was not entering the sites in chronological order. Since the filling of the ditch does not appear to have been disturbed, this raises the intriguing possibility that these artefacts were being taken from another, unlocated deposit.

Why is this so revealing? It seems likely that a proportion of this material – most specifically the Beaker pottery – was already of considerable age when it was deposited at Site IV. That may also apply to the earlier Neolithic artefacts that were found there, and yet there is compelling evidence that such material was placed in the ditch with some formality. The same is also true of the animal bones associated with them.

It is clear that the detailed distribution of Beaker pottery in the ditch of Site IV

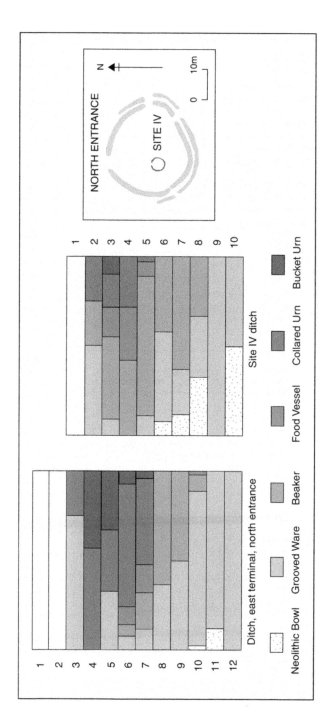

Figure 37 The pottery sequences on two of the excavated sites at Mount Pleasant, Dorset, England, according to the layers defined in the field

Source: Information from Wainwright 1979a and Thomas 1996

also conflicts with conventional chronological schemes. Supposedly successive styles are found in the same levels, and the distribution of this material has little in common with the orthodox sequence. At this point we might be tempted to reject these chronological models entirely. We would be encouraged to do so by a series of radiocarbon dates for British Beaker pottery, for these entirely failed to support the usual ordering of these vessels based on their typology and associations (Kinnes *et al.* 1991). Some of the pots associated with radiocarbon dates were much later than had been expected (Figure 38).

That raises certain difficulties, for Bell Beakers are by no means an insular phenomenon and many of the individual types have counterparts on the Continent, and in particular in the Netherlands, where a similar dating programme has been undertaken (Lanting and Van der Waals 1981). This supports the conventional sequence, on which the British scheme had been based, but it also raises a further possibility. The radiocarbon dates for British Beakers – including those from Mount Pleasant itself – are dating the deposition of these vessels. It is simply an assumption that such dates can also be used to fix the time of their production, and the two very different stratigraphic sequences at Mount Pleasant suggest that this is an assumption that cannot be made. Quite simply, the material deposited around the timber circle at Mount Pleasant – and very likely the material from

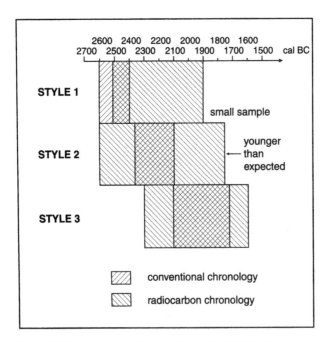

Figure 38 The conventional chronology of British Beaker pottery
according to the styles defined in Case 1993,
compared with the results of radiocarbon dating

other monuments and graves subjected to radiocarbon dating – was already of some considerable age when it was committed to the ground. (For a similar argument see Harrison *et al.* 1999.) If that is right, then the structured deposits inside British monuments may have yet another dimension. The material that was being used may refer not only to distant places but also to distant times. At a much earlier date, there is a parallel for this in the first phase of Stonehenge, where high-precision radiocarbon dating suggests that some of the bones in the ditch may have been up to 200 years old when they were deposited there (Cleal *et al.* 1995: 529–31).

To sum up, the monuments of the later Neolithic period provided a structure according to which existing traditions of deposition could be organised. They offered a framework that allowed different kinds of material to be deposited in relation to one another, and their architecture ensured that these would need to be experienced in a prescribed order. At the same time, these deposits had to be interpreted not only in terms of their relationship with other collections on the same site, but also in relation to their wider references. Some of them may have referred to areas beyond the bounds of the settled landscape, such as the collections of red deer bones found in Orkney, whilst others may have evoked connections with far off places where the artefacts themselves began their lives. Here the obvious example is the use of stone axes imported from remote quarries in the highlands. In certain cases, it even seems likely that these artefacts were being returned to the elements from which they were formed. This is obvious in the case of carved chalk, but there are subtler examples too, such as the circulation of human bones between settlements and other sites or even the recycling of Grooved Ware and Beakers through the use of grog. On one level, that last practice extended the lifespan of individual vessels, for they were used to make other pots. On another, there seems to have been a willingness to keep these artefacts in being after their useful life was apparently over. This certainly seems to be the case with the vessels of Grooved Ware that had been carefully mended, and it is surely the explanation for the eccentric chronology of Beaker pottery at Mount Pleasant and other sites. In each case, the symbolic significance of the material that was being offered extended back into the past.

That seems especially appropriate if the sequences of deposits brought together at these monuments were formed – or inspected – in the course of framing a narrative. By their very nature, origin myths lead from the past to the present, and from the exotic to the familiar. I suggest that the monuments of later Neolithic Britain capitalised on the symbolism encoded in so many different deposits and provided it with a more comprehensive structure. They introduced a range of symbolically charged materials into a new architectural setting, and in doing so they added to their meanings and imbued them with a greater formality. By bringing together elements that were otherwise deposited in quite different kinds of locations, these earthworks, and the buildings within them, eventually became a microcosm of the landscape as a whole.

Chapter 9

Walking on water

A case study from Bronze Age Scandinavia

This chapter discusses the changing relationship between rock carvings and funerary monuments in the landscape of Scandinavia. They seem to form part of a single system that has important elements in common with the cosmology of Arctic hunter gatherers and also with recent interpretations of the iconography of Bronze Age rock art and metal finds. The discussion focuses on the changing significance attached to ships, water, islands and hills in prehistoric systems of belief, and on the ways in which they found expression in the construction of funerary cairns and the creation of rock art.

At the water's edge

It is difficult to date the images in Scandinavian rock art. In a few cases, the carvings depict objects with a well-established chronology, but sometimes the relationship is the other way round, so that bronze artefacts are decorated with motifs that also appear in petroglyphs. These are quite unusual. The best way of achieving at least a relative chronology is through the study of shoreline displacement, and this provides the basis for the more convincing regional sequences found in this part of the world.

The principle behind these schemes is very simple. After the last glaciation, the ice caps gradually melted. The land no longer bore their weight, and its level rose. This happened to different extents and at different rates from one region to another. The position of the coast was further out and old shorelines became dry land. It was a process that could last for millennia. As a result, it is possible to record changes of sea level on a local basis (Bertilsson 1987; Helsgog 1988).

The importance of this finding is that rock art appears to have been created on the ancient shoreline. To some extent, this may have happened because the rock had been worn smooth by ice and water. It remained free of vegetation, while inland areas were gradually colonised by trees. That hypothesis provides the basis for developing a relative sequence of art styles. The method suggests the *earliest possible dates* at which particular surfaces might have become available for carving. Assuming that the images were created as close as possible to the water's edge, the oldest carvings should be those at the greatest elevation, and progressively younger designs ought to be found lower down. That is because the higher parts of these exposures would have been the first to emerge. As the land rose and the coastline retreated, new expanses of rock would be exposed and these could be decorated. The result is a sequence that is the exact opposite of that familiar in excavation, where the youngest deposits are at the surface and the oldest are underneath them.

It is important to recognise that all this method can do is to suggest maximum ages for particular panels of rock art. There is no reason why younger images should not have been superimposed on older carvings or why they could not have been made well above the water's edge. There are some cases in which carvings of different ages cut across one another, but these are not particularly common. The usual pattern is for different styles of depiction to be distributed at different heights above sea level. This provides a reason for accepting this method of analysis, but unless there is some explanation why new carvings *had to be* at the water's edge, it is easy to become trapped in a circular argument.

This question has recently been addressed by Helsgog (1997), who suggests a number of reasons why rock carvings needed to be created in this position. The purely practical arguments are insufficient – some designs were created on most unsuitable surfaces, and in any case many areas were never invaded by trees – and he prefers an interpretation based on the ethnography of northern hunter gatherers. In traditional cosmologies, the shoreline is the meeting place of three quite different worlds, each of which has a specific identity and associations. It is where the land meets the sea, but it is also where both these elements confront the sky (Figure 39). The distinction is especially important because, in Arctic tradition, the sea is associated with the dead. Perhaps the rock carvings were in liminal locations where it would be possible to communicate between the different domains. Ethnographic accounts suggest that this was the role of the shaman. Cataracts were important too. They were where the cosmic river provided access to the dead, and that may be why they attracted large numbers of rock carvings. The images may have been made in places where different worlds came together, and these locations could have acted as ceremonial centres (Tilley 1991a: Chapters 9 and 10).

Very similar beliefs are recorded across a wide area, extending from the north of Russia, through Scandinavia to Canada, but it is not clear whether they were once shared by populations living further to the south. Helsgog himself applies this interpretation to hunters' art and suggests that there were important changes as the conventions of farmers' rock art were adopted in areas further to the north. On the other hand, there may be evidence of similar beliefs in southern Scandinavia, although initially these were expressed in a different form.

There the association between the sea and the dead may go back to the Ertebolle phase. Although the sample of finds is very small, there is clear evidence for the burial of the dead in boats from the Mesolithic and Neolithic periods. Excavated graves seem to have contained canoes, whilst intact burials have been found underwater (Skaarup 1995). That same association was maintained during the Bronze Age, when a series of ship settings were used for cremation burials

Figure 39 The coastal setting of the prehistoric rock art at Vingen, western Norway
Source: Trond Lødøen

(Capelle 1995; Strömberg 1961). The earlier of these settings of stones were buried under cairns, but in the Late Bronze Age there were other sites where the same design was rendered above ground (Artelius 1996). These are probably the precursors of the better-known Iron Age ship settings, and ultimately of some of the rich boat burials of the Migration period.

It is not just that southern Scandinavia had a tradition of boat burial that recalls the northern association between the sea and death. In fact, many of the rock carvings in that region were just as strongly connected with the shoreline. Indeed, when related images were created in northern Scandinavia, they could still be found on the water's edge. There are other indications that the carvings of ships were associated with the dead, although this is not to suggest that it was their only meaning. There are sites in southern Scandinavia where ships are actually depicted on burial cists, and at Lugnaso in Sweden there was another drawing of a boat facing one of these structures. It was located inside a ship setting buried beneath a circular cairn and dated from the Late Bronze Age (Strömberg 1961: 90–5).

There are other drawings of ships on bronze artefacts, and these have been used to date those in the landscape (Kaul 1995). They are found mainly on razors, although they extend to weapons, ornaments and other personal items. This is particularly interesting, because these razors are usually found with cremation burials, although the objects themselves do not seem to have passed through the fire. It has been suggested that the razors and other utensils had been used to prepare the corpse for the funeral; they were not grave goods in the usual sense of the term (Treherne 1995: 121). Razors with drawings of ships are most commonly found in Denmark (Figure 40; Dotzler 1984: 120–9), whilst the same motif occurs in the rock art of Sweden and Norway (Malmer 1981). Their distributions complement one another so neatly that they may have had the same significance. The association between the sea and death was widely shared, although it might have been expressed in different ways in different regions.

In fact, there are some cases in which rock carvings of ships are explicitly opposed to images related to the land. This has been recognised by Burenhult (1980) in his study of the rock carvings of southern Sweden. The drawings of ships are closer to the prehistoric shoreline than those depicting vehicles and footsoles. In the decorated cist beneath the Early Bronze Age cairn at Kivik in Scania, the carvings of boats were opposite scenes set on land, depicting a chariot and a procession (Randsborg 1993). In Randsborg's reconstruction, the carvings with the boats would have faced out to sea and the other group would have faced inland.

He also suggests that the carved panels at Kivik epitomise the vertical ordering of the world. These images invite us to consider the landscape as a whole. Within the structure of the cist, he identifies:

> a schematic division denoting the three cosmic spheres of the Bronze Age: Above, the world of light (thereby the sun) and the human world. . . . Below this follows 'nature' in the form of creatures subordinate to man. At the bottom, the land of the moon, night (and death). . . . The Kivik imagery probably holds yet another cosmological and hitherto unrecognised dimension, which seems to correspond to the fundamental structure of a 'shamanic' . . . conception of the world: a nether country with the sea of the dead, followed by the land of the living, and above this the heavens.
>
> (Randsborg 1993: 119–20)

He finds the same structure in the decorated kerb of another barrow at Sagaholm.

Figure 40 Danish Bronze Age razors with drawings of ships
Source: After Kaul 1995

There is some common ground between this reading of the imagery at Kivik and Kaul's reconstruction of prehistoric cosmology, as evidenced by the decorated metalwork of Bronze Age Denmark. In his interpretation, a ship draws the sun across the sky. At different stages in the cycle, it is assisted by a horse, a snake and a fish. Since this analysis is concerned with quite different material from Randsborg's study, it is striking that in Kaul's scheme the passage of the sun during the night – its absence from the world, in a sense its *death* – is associated with a fish (Kaul 1997). Again, this recalls the association between the sea and the dead that is such a characteristic of northern mythology.

These interpretations suggest that at least some of the ideas that Helsgog takes from Arctic ethnography may have a certain relevance to the rock art of southern Scandinavia. Randsborg's interpretation of the Kivik cist is especially relevant here, for it combines a cosmological understanding of the imagery with its placing in the local landscape. If the organisation of the motifs recalls the distinctions between the land, the sea and the sky, their locations within the burial chamber can be explained in terms of the actual topography of the site: the carvings of ships face towards the water, whilst the panel showing a procession is directed towards the land. It suggests a framework for studies extending across a wider area. Can we consider the placing of the images in relation to the siting of rock art as a whole? For such an analysis to succeed, it will need to be undertaken in a landscape whose archaeology is already well recorded.

The isles of the dead

The type of analysis outlined above is most likely to be achieved in the region with the greatest density of rock art, although it would be quite wrong to extend any detailed interpretation from that area to other parts of Scandinavia. This study is concerned with Bohuslän on the west coast of Sweden, not far from the border with Norway. This is a major focus of what has been called farmers' art, which dates from between about 1800 and 500 BC (Bertilsson 1987; Nordbladh 1980). Many of the decorated surfaces seem to have built up gradually over this period, but only a few individual elements can be dated through the use of similar decorative devices on artefacts. Bertilsson suggests that most of the motifs belong to the later part of this period. The subject matter of the carvings consists of a fairly limited repertoire of images, in which the main elements in order of frequency are: cup marks (the commonest), then ships, human figures, animals, wheeled vehicles and footprints. Although a few panels might show scenes from daily life – there are illustrations of hunting and ploughing – their juxtaposition with other images suggests that they should be understood metaphorically. These include gigantic men wearing horns, wild animals and abstract signs. There is an explicit emphasis on masculinity. Tim Yates (1993) has shown that most of the figures depicted with weapons are explicitly phallic, and sometimes they are shown together with deer carrying a full set of antlers. One context for these drawings, he says, may be initiation ceremonies.

The argument is plausible but refers to nothing beyond the art itself. That is the great frustration of studying this kind of material. Scandinavian rock art is found in the open air and, as a result, the carved surfaces are very rarely associated with other evidence of activity. The art forms part of the prehistoric landscape, yet it is impossible to interpret it in a wider setting unless we can relate its features to further components of the archaeological record. Without this relationship, it is a private preserve in which one interpretation is as good as any other.

In Bohuslän, prehistorians have long recognised the need to study this distinctive material in relation to other features of the landscape. The difficulty has been in deciding which elements to use. Two kinds of analysis have seemed particularly attractive.

The first emphasises the close relationship between these sites, with their numerous drawings of ships, and the prehistoric coastline. It is an interpretation that has its advocates in many parts of Scandinavia, but along the dissected coast of Bohuslän it is easy to see why this idea is so attractive. The carvings are not located on the modern coast, but instead occur in a compact zone running parallel to it between about 5 and 15 km (3 and 9 miles) inland. Some of the greatest concentrations of carvings are found towards the heads of shallow valleys that lead down to the sea (Figure 41).

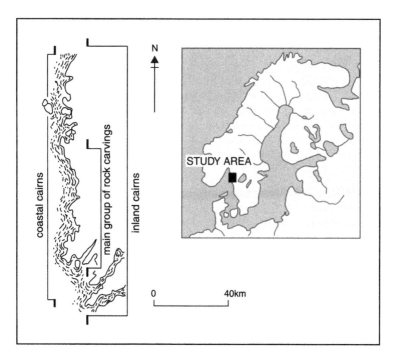

Figure 41 The distribution of Bronze Age rock art and burial cairns in Bohuslän, western Sweden

There is no doubt that the majority of carvings were situated on former shore-lines. The level of the land has been rising since the last Ice Age, and the sea has been in retreat. In the late Mesolithic period, the shoreline was at about 25 m (82 ft) above its level today. By the beginning of the Bronze Age, it may have fallen to 15 m (49 ft), and by the end of the period it was roughly 8 m (26 ft) (Bertilsson 1987: Chapter 7). Nearly all the carvings are found on panels of rock around the edges of the lowland, and in most cases there are hills or larger outcrops behind them.

There are two main problems in making this equation. First, the evidence of the ships may have been taken too literally. It is obviously tempting to relate the drawings of boats to the importance of sea transport in such a dissected topog-raphy, especially when bronze itself had to be introduced to Scandinavia from areas further to the south. It is all too easy to read this emphasis on ships as a reference to the importance of contacts with distant areas (Malmer 1981). On the other hand, we have already seen that in Scandinavian archaeology, ships and boats also play a role in funeral rites from the Mesolithic period to the Middle Ages (Crumlin-Pedersen and Thye 1995). It may be inappropriate to consider the ship carvings in terms of the everyday.

At the same time, the correlation between the placing of the rock carvings and the Bronze Age shoreline has perhaps been overemphasised, for in fact sea levels were already falling when these drawings were first created (Bertilsson 1987: Chapter 7). This means that some of the drawings of ships overlooked areas of dry land, whilst others were still being made on or close to the shoreline. Accord-ing to both Nordbladh and Bertilsson, the silts left behind by the retreating waters were among the most productive parts of the local landscape, and they appear to have been where Bronze Age settlements were established. The rock carvings occur in local concentrations along the junction between the areas vacated by the sea and the hills that had always been above the water. That is not to say that the sea had reached its present position by the end of the Bronze Age, for it is likely that it continued to recede during this period. It seems entirely probable that the local population were aware of this process.

Somewhat paradoxically, there is very little evidence that similar carvings were created where the coast of Bohuslän met the open sea. In fact, it appears that a more complex process was at work. In those areas that had once been occupied by the sea, we find large numbers of rock carvings, including drawings of ships. Rock art of any kind is more sparsely represented along the Bronze Age shoreline further to the west.

Now we turn to the second, very different attempt to relate the distribution of the rock art to an important feature of the prehistoric landscape. The coast of Bohuslän contains a dense distribution of Bronze Age burial cairns. These vary from fairly informal monuments to quite massive constructions, the largest of which are found on small islands in the coastal archipelago. These islands are by no means extensive and some of them would be unlikely to sustain a resident population. The larger cairns form a chain extending along the west coast of

Sweden and provide striking landmarks for sailors in these waters. Again, they have played their part in reconstructions of seaborne trade in the Bronze Age (Kristiansen 1987).

The distribution of these cairns extends inland, where it overlaps with that of the rock carvings. The two features seem to be found in a consistent relationship to one another, so that the cairns are almost invariably on the higher ground, separated from the fertile lowland soils by the distribution of petroglyphs. Although rock art and burial cairns are sometimes found very close together, there is usually sufficient evidence to suggest that the landscape was divided into two zones. Nordbladh (1980) has argued that the carved rocks define the outer edges of the domestic landscape and divide them from the domain of the dead on the higher ground. If so, it seems entirely reasonable to infer that the rock art may have been created or used in the course of funerary ritual.

The subdivision of the landscape by height recalls the traditional cosmologies found in areas further to the north, where the Saami distinguish between the sky, the land and the sea, and consider some of the rocks and hills to possess special powers. Again this attractive correlation seems to break down. Although the spatial relationship between rock art and Bronze Age cairns is consistent and generally persuasive, this is so only in inland areas. As we have seen, the burial monuments extend to the coast, where fewer carvings are found. Indeed, it is on the small islands off the coast itself that the largest cairns were built. That means that the drawings of boats are found in one part of the landscape where funerary monuments are recorded, but in the very areas where the dead would be taken across the water such images are rare or even absent. The chronology of the carvings and cairns certainly overlaps, as both may belong mainly to the Later Bronze Age (Bertilsson 1987). It is because the two distributions coincide to such a limited extent that not everyone accepts that the petroglyphs were associated with the dead.

At first sight, then, it seems as if each attempt to interpret west Swedish rock art in relation to the wider landscape has its weaknesses. On the one hand, many of the ship carvings are near to former shorelines, but some of them were not created until those areas had been abandoned by the sea. On the other hand, a number of the burial cairns are on the rocky prominences enclosed by Bronze Age rock carvings, but more examples are found on islands, where these designs do not appear.

Perhaps there is a way of reconciling these arguments and of interpreting the rock art in a wider context. This approach depends on one further characteristic of these sites. For the most part, the images are organised in relation to a viewer who is looking uphill from the relict shoreline. In terms of Norbladh's hypothesis, that viewer is observing the carvings from the zone occupied by the living and is also looking outwards towards the domain of the dead. The majority of the motifs are organised according to that perspective and are arranged in a horizontal plane on the surface of the rock (Figure 42). That argument extends to nearly all the major motifs but especially to the humans, animals and boats. The latter are more

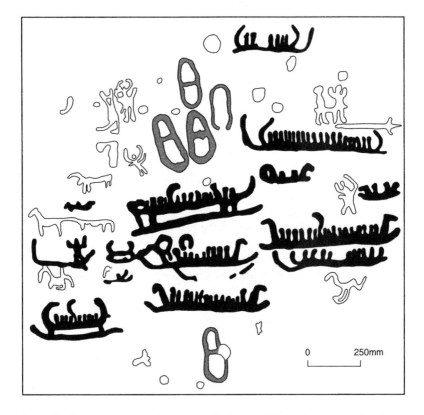

Figure 42 Part of a decorated panel in Kville hundred, Bohuslän, western Sweden
Source: Data from Fredsjö 1981

often found than other naturalistic images, and in the one area with a comprehensive series of published records (Fredsjö 1971, 1975 and 1981) it is clear that on 80 per cent of the carved surfaces these vessels extend along the contours. In only 14 per cent of the panels are boats drawn at right angles to them, and on another 6 per cent they seem to cross them obliquely.

The drawings of boats stand out from all the others because so many of these vessels were portrayed. At some of the largest sites, they amount to entire fleets that occupy a compact zone running along the contours of the rock. They are usually interspersed with the other motifs, but occasionally they divide particular images on the lower slopes of the rock from those towards its upper limits. For instance, there are sites where cup marks are concentrated towards the base of the rock, whilst beyond the zone of ship carvings are occasional hunting scenes, groups of wild animals and drawings of phallic men who are dancing or fighting.

It would be wrong to make too much of that division, for it is perhaps more important to reconsider the significance of the ships themselves – the commonest of all the motifs apart from cup marks. One contribution of recent research on prehistoric art is to emphasise the sheer range of meanings that may attach to any particular image (Tilley 1991a). It is to that plurality of meanings that such symbols owe their power. There is no need to reject any of the interpretations that I have summarised so far – ships may evoke notions of foreign travel; they may well depict the journey of the dead – but it is also possible to suggest an interpretation of their placing in this particular landscape.

The sheer abundance of the images, many of them pursuing the same course along the contours of the rock, is the single most striking impression provided by these sites. At one level they consist of many separate drawings, which perhaps accumulated over a considerable period of time, but at another level they seem to form a boundary dividing the viewer on the lower ground from the upper part of the rock and the entire area beyond it. It is the fact that so many ships should follow the same axis that makes these drawings so convincing. In such cases, they may be shown crossing the same stretch of water, for unlike the surface of the earth the sea appears to be level.

There is one natural extension of this observation, but it does not seem to have been suggested before. Maybe the presence of so many ships was not just a reference to their importance in the life of the community; perhaps they were depicted in this particular way *to convey the idea of water itself.* The drawings recreated the sea at the foot of the high ground by depicting the ships on its surface. More than that, the sheer abundance of carved rocks around the edges of the lowlands allowed a mythological landscape to be constructed in which the rocky hills and outcrops that overlooked the settled land could be interpreted as islands, just like those on the coast. Where such islands really existed, their edges would be self-evident, but where inland features were accorded the same significance, it was necessary to describe their limits by depicting an area of open water. That was achieved most effectively by drawings of ships.

If that argument has any merit, it simplifies some of the interpretations that I discussed at the start of this section. It is no longer necessary to distinguish between the cairns that were built on islands and those in inland areas bounded by a zone of rock carvings, for the effect of those drawings was to convert the higher ground into another group of islands, where the dead might be commemorated. Hills and outcrops that might actually have been islands long before these carvings were made were turned into islands again by the use of these images (Figure 43).

That hypothesis might explain one final observation. I said that the organisation of the carvings presupposes a viewer on the lower ground, for virtually all the images follow a horizontal plane. Some of the wheeled vehicles do not conform to this convention, but the only common motif that flouts it entirely is the footprint or footsole. These images generally appear in pairs and are usually, but not always, provided with shoes. On 77 per cent of the carved surfaces, they follow a path leading up (and down) the surface of the rock. In this way, they cut across the zone of ships and other images and connect the lower ground where the

111111111

settlements seem to have been with the hills where the dead were buried. In fact, they depict a movement *in both directions*, as if these were the only paths that permitted communication between those two areas. Most of the tracks lead towards the lower ground, and in one sense they transgress the expanse of water that was depicted on these rocks and link the 'islands' of the dead with the domain of the living and the sea.

The footprints are carved at life size, but this is not true of any of the humans or animals depicted on these rocks. Despite the fact that people might be shown at a variety of different scales, none of them could have left these tracks: nor are the figures located on the carved surface according to these paths. *Those who left these trails are entirely invisible.* Either they have moved beyond the limits of the rock, or else they have no bodies at all. Are they the dead? There is some reason to think so. In the mythology of northern Scandinavia, the dead occupy an underworld that is the mirror image of the world occupied by the living: 'the lower layer [of the cosmos] is the inverted world of the dead, whose feet, since they walk upside-down, are sometimes thought ... to touch the soles of the living who walk upright' (Ingold 1986: 246). The footwear depicted in the carvings may also be relevant here, for in Icelandic mythology the recently dead must be helped on their journey to the other world by the provision of special gear known as *hel-shoes* (Ellis 1943: 39, 62 and 75). Could this be an echo of the beliefs enshrined in Bronze Age rock art? If so, the liminal area in between the living and the dead might be the appropriate place for rituals to be undertaken. I do not suggest that such ceremonies were restricted to mortuary rites.

This interpretation shares some common ground with the cosmological scheme described by Helsgog (1997) in areas further to the north and postulated by

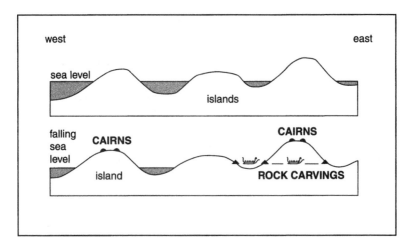

Figure 43 The siting of burial cairns and rock art in Bohuslän, western Sweden, in relation to prehistoric changes of sea level

Randsborg (1993) towards the southern limit of the distribution of Scandinavian rock art. The carvings in Bohuslän are located close to the sea, often on former shorelines, and include numerous drawings of ships. Above them, on the higher ground, there are burial cairns, whilst more of these monuments are found on the small islands off the coast. In Arctic ethnography, such islands are associated with the dead. Ships may have similar associations. In southern Scandinavia, they can be depicted inside burial cists and they are also shown on the razors that sometimes accompanied the dead. The same symbolism extends from the canoe burials of the Mesolithic and Neolithic periods to the ship settings of the Bronze and Iron Ages. On a metaphysical plane, they expressed the journey taken by the dead to another world, but boats would also have been used to convey the corpse from the mainland of western Sweden to its burial place in the coastal archipelago. As well as the ships, there were footprints, and I have made the suggestion that these recorded the passage of the deceased from the cairns on the higher ground, through a liminal area marked by drawings of ships and down to the sea itself.

To some extent, this interpretation was suggested by Randsborg's analysis of the decorated cist at Kivik. It is unfortunate that at present it cannot be developed in more detail in relation to excavated cairns in Bohuslän, but there is another site in Scania where these ideas can be taken further. Twenty km (12½ miles) from Kivik are the well-known rock carvings of Järrestad 4 (Coles 1999). Like Kivik, they include drawings of people riding horses – albeit in a rather different style – and there is another decorated slab from a cist very near to that site (Althin 1945, Vol. 1: 71–2).

The carvings at Järrestad occupy a large sheet of sloping rock overlooking a small basin and a valley that extends down to the modern coast. The highest point on the rock is occupied by the remains of two mounds, the survivors of what was once a group of three (Althin 1945, Vol. 1: 80–91 and Vol. 2: 44–66). They were investigated over 100 years ago and contained a number of urned cremations as well as finds of Late Bronze Age metalwork of Periods V and VI. One of the barrows also included a large cup-marked stone (Althin 1945 Vol. 1, 81–9). Not far from this site was a cist containing a slab depicting two ships sailing in opposite directions to one another. According to Kaul's interpretation, this would symbolise the night (Althin 1945, Vol. 1: 71–2; Kaul 1997).

There are more drawings of ships on the rock outcrop at Järrestad, as well as human figures and cup marks, but the most striking features of this site are the drawings of footsoles and footprints (Figure 44). As in Bohuslän, these extend across the contours of the rock so that they provide a link between the summit of the outcrop and a small bog below. The zone of footsoles extends across the entire distribution of motifs, at right angles to the drawings of ships. Some of the footsoles are paired, and virtually all of them seem to follow a path leading towards the lower ground. The footprints, on the other hand, occur in four main concentrations around the edges of the carved surface, although some isolated examples overlap with the distribution of footsoles. A few of these point upslope

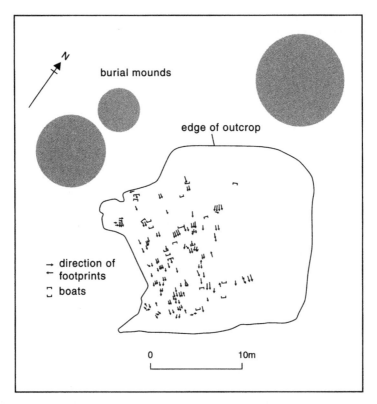

Figure 44 The relationship between the panel of rock art at Järrestad site 4,
Scania, southern Sweden, and the adjacent barrow cemetery
Source: Based on information from Althin 1945, Burenhult 1980, Coles 1999
and a site visit in 1998

or along the contours, but again the majority lead downhill. Rather unusually, some of the drawings of ships emphasise the view from the higher ground and could be understood only by people looking towards the valley bottom. The remainder follow the normal pattern and presuppose an audience facing the crest of the outcrop.

On one level, this arrangement recalls Nordbladh's evidence from Bohuslän: the tracks lead up and down the rock, at right angles to the drawings of ships. They also lead between the area above the carvings and the damp ground below them. Further down the valley was the sea. But in this case there is one vital difference, for the footprints extend almost to the summit of the outcrop where the Bronze Age monuments were built. It seems as if the main line of footsoles ended at, or just beside, a small mound that has now disappeared. This monument was associated with a burial dating from Period VI which included a twisted bronze neckring, two pendants and a pin (Althin 1945). The other footsoles and footprints are not so closely related to individual barrows, but they do seem to lead out of the cemetery towards a bog or pool.

Here the pattern that I have suggested for Bohuslän is compressed into a limited space, so that it appears that the tracks left by the footsoles originate *in the barrow cemetery itself.* They run downslope from the graves, following a course that could ultimately have led to the sea. Some of the drawings of ships suggest the same interpretation, as they could have been observed only by someone looking *down the surface of the rock.* The link between the open-air carvings and the burials is reinforced by the drawing of ships found in a cist nearby.

If we follow Randsborg's reading of the imagery at Kivik and Sagaholm, we might envisage a path cutting across the landscape of the living and linking two distinct domains: the higher ground, the 'heavens', where Bronze Age barrows celebrated the ancestors, and the sea of the dead to which they had to travel. If the footsoles do represent the *hel-shoes* of the recently deceased, they may record the path from the grave to the world beyond.

Some of the same elements can be found in a poem by the seventeenth-century mystic Thomas Traherne. This recalls a number of the observations on which this study has been based:

> By walking Men's reversed Feet
> I chanc'd another world to meet;
> Tho it did not to View exceed
> A Phantom, 'tis a World indeed,
> > Where Skies beneath us shine
> > And Earth by Art divine
> Another face presents below,
> Where People's feet against Ours go.
>
> 'Shadows in the Water', Traherne 1903

Coda

This study has considered a small part of an enormous body of material. It has been concerned with the rock art of only two areas of Sweden – Scania and Bohuslän – and has offered one possible interpretation of their significance. Moreover, much of this discussion has been concerned with just two of the individual motifs: the footsole and the boat. Rock art might have been used in very different ways in other regions of Scandinavia – and it probably was. It would be wrong to make excessive claims on behalf of this analysis.

One reason for expressing such caution is that art is frequently polysemous: it does not have a single meaning at all. Graphic images are so powerful precisely because they can bring so many different concepts together and can convey several levels of significance at the same time. That is something that spoken language is poorly equipped to do. It is perfectly possible that other interpretations of

Scandinavian rock art have the same validity; indeed, many different positions could have an element of truth behind them. I do not say this in order to be fashionable, but because it is the very nature of visual art to convey several messages simultaneously. So much depends on the contexts in which people encountered it and on what they were allowed to know. This account picks out one theme among many and considers its importance.

Although this chapter has been concerned with rock art, the main implications of this study are for landscape archaeology. Whilst this particular interpretation depends on recognising certain visual images, it is my contention that they can be understood only by setting them in a wider context. One such context was provided by the ethnohistory of Arctic hunter gatherers, but another was suggested by the placing of the rock art in the natural terrain. Neither was sufficient in itself, but taken in combination they suggested some directions that research might follow. The rock art could not be interpreted without the evidence of the burial cairns. The ship carvings would make little sense without the evidence of decorated metalwork and its associations, and the changing configuration of the cultural landscape would remain entirely mysterious without the insights provided by environmental archaeology. Take any of these elements away, and the entire edifice collapses.

We have been following footprints across the surface of a rock, and have come to the conclusion that the people who made them were invisible. There are times when that could be a description of archaeology itself.

Chapter 10

A long-playing record

The significance of natural places in later prehistoric Europe

What can we conclude from these analyses? The final chapter is a more general account of how natural places were used in Europe from the Mesolithic period to the early Middle Ages. It reconsiders the suggestion that the people who built great monuments appropriated the powers originally associated with these locations, suggesting that in fact there was a constant interplay between the two kinds of site. The creation of monuments did not reduce the significance attached to natural places in the landscape, although it was gradually transformed. They retained their importance until, at various times between the Iron Age and the early medieval period, they were caught up in the political processes that led to the emergence of the state.

Acknowledging the boundaries

Boundaries provoke various responses from archaeologists. Theorists have paid them particular attention. Boundaries between artefact styles have a special role in studies of ethnicity, whilst the same word has taken on a further range of meanings in the analysis of material culture (Hodder 1982a). Sharp distinctions in the forms or associations of artefacts may relate to other important divisions in the past, such as those between men and women, young and old, the initiated and uninitiated. At times, the term takes on a life all of its own, so that 'boundedness' in pottery decoration becomes a metaphor that refers to the differences between people in society (Hodder 1982b). In the end, the concept can hardly take the strain.

If there are boundaries in the mind, there are boundaries on the ground as well, but these do not seem to have attracted much attention in field archaeology. I have argued that in earlier prehistory landscape studies are still dominated by monuments rather than places, so that large areas are overlooked. In later prehistory, the situation remains much the same. Although entire landscapes have been surveyed, excavation still concentrates on the settlement sites. The boundaries that can be identified on the ground are largely ignored.

When a project does focus on ancient boundaries, the results can be revealing. The Wessex Linear Ditches Project is a case in point. This was undertaken by Roy

Entwistle, Frances Raymond and the writer between 1988 and 1991. It had a fairly conventional research design. The aims of the project were to establish the form and date of a number of the earthwork boundaries on Salisbury Plain, to study their roles in the ancient landscape and to advise on how these features might be preserved. The field methods used were quite conventional too. The earthworks were traced on the ground and were excavated on a small scale where artefacts could be recognised on the surface or where the relationship between the ditches and features such as field systems was to be investigated. This work was combined with molluscan analysis and radiocarbon dating (Bradley *et al.* 1994).

In this particular area, it became clear that the ditches had originally been dug during the Late Bronze Age and that they enclosed a number of distinct territories, each of which was dominated by a large open settlement. Some of the earthworks were retained in an Iron Age landscape of enclosures and hill forts, and at this stage certain of the boundary ditches were recut, whilst others were ploughed over or allowed to go out of use. The sequence was at an end by the later part of the Iron Age, although there are other regions in which the first land boundaries were earlier in date or where they retained their importance over an even longer period.

Although excavation had quite specific objectives, it was still capable of presenting some surprises. In four different cases, the lower levels of these boundaries preserved unexpected evidence of structured deposits, all of them dating from the Iron Age. We examined the terminals of two of these ditches, which ended just outside the defences of Sidbury hill fort. In one case, there was a human skull accompanied by a few other bones, and in the end of the other ditch was a cattle skull. Similar deposits were found at further points along the boundary system. On one site, there was a horse skull, and elsewhere there was a second cattle skull, lacking its lower jaw (Figure 45; Bradley *et al.* 1994: 42, 46, 53 and 57). The very small scale of our excavations – just thirty narrow sections through ditches that extend for many kilometres – suggests that originally such finds were very common.

The discovery of placed deposits in the ditches on Salisbury Plain has wider implications that it was not possible to explore in the original report on this project. Similar finds are recognised at Iron Age hill forts and enclosures in southern England, and there are indications that comparable material is associated with other occupation sites (Hill 1995). This had always been interpreted in relation to the functioning of the settlements, so much so that it had been thought of as domestic waste. Now the same kinds of deposits were being found at some remove from the settlements, and in a quite different kind of context. At the same time, more detailed analysis of Bronze Age and Iron Age river finds was showing that this material did not consist entirely of fine metalwork. Excavation at sites like Flag Fen and Eton Rowing Lake was bringing to light human and animal skulls and other bones (Pryor 1992; Tim Allen pers. comm.). As we become more aware of the archaeological potential of rivers, further examples of this phenomenon are coming to light.

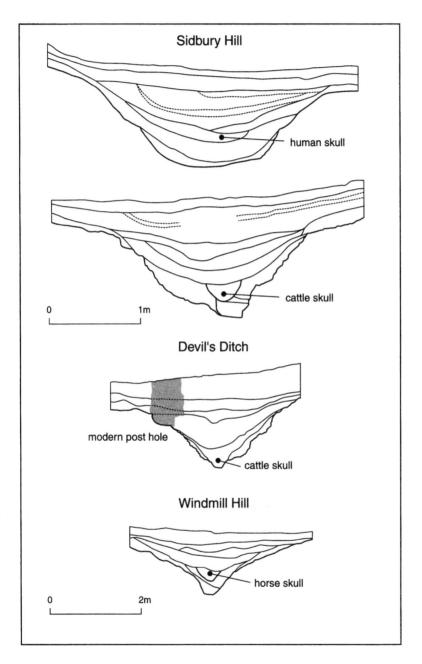

Figure 45 The contexts of human and animal bone deposits in the fillings of
Wessex linear ditches
Source: Information from Bradley, Entwistle and Raymond 1994

On one level, then, the human and animal skulls found in the land boundaries on Salisbury Plain resembled the material deposited at settlement sites: a practice that is a particular feature of the Early and Middle Iron Ages. On another level, they recalled a longer tradition of wetland deposits that certainly extended as far back as the British Early Bronze Age and most probably originated in the Neolithic (Bradley 1990). The finds from the linear ditches occupied a pivotal position in that sequence. Taken together, the individual deposits have radiocarbon dates that span the full extent of the Iron Age. This is especially revealing as it was at this time that the quantity of metalwork deposited in watery locations was at its minimum (Bradley 1990a: Chapter 4). Instead, it seems as if deposits on dry land assumed a greater prominence. They also had a quite different composition. They emphasised the fertility of the human and animal populations and were closely connected with the agricultural cycle (Hill 1995).

The discovery of these deposits in linear boundaries adds more detail to this scheme. The question of *time* is all-important here. The boundaries were created in a landscape that already had a long history. They seem to have been laid out between a series of Early Bronze Age round barrows in a manner that suggests that particular burial mounds still held a special significance when these earthworks were constructed. The ditches did not necessarily run between the most conspicuous landmarks, and sometimes changed direction to incorporate barrows that could not be identified from any distance away (Bradley *et al*. 1994: 141). In that sense, the linear ditches may have been following older divisions in the landscape, divisions whose significance was ensured by the presence of the dead. At the same time, the placed deposits of human and animal skulls were not an original feature of the earthwork boundaries, as all of them were found within *recut* ditches. The original layout of these boundaries is probably Late Bronze Age, but the deposits all date from the Iron Age. The precise form of their earthworks is of more than passing interest, for it was at this time that many of them were converted from flat-bottomed ditches to ditches with a sharp V profile (Bradley *et al*. 1994: 67–8). This is exactly the structural sequence that is observed at hill forts over the same period (Cunliffe 1991: Chapter 14). It seems as if the outward form of the land boundaries was changed in order to conform to the conventions adopted on those sites. It seems hardly surprising that both groups of earthworks should be associated with offerings of the same kind.

In fact, it is quite likely that the material associated with the enclosed settlements also changed its character. In Wessex, it seems as if fragmentary human bones are mainly a feature of Early Iron Age sites and that the number of intact bodies increased during later phases (Figure 46). Where they occur together, for example in the enclosure at Winnal Down, single bones can be associated with the perimeter and complete skeletons are found within these sites (Hill 1995: Chapter 9). At the same time, finds of animal skulls and long bones occur in the boundaries of early enclosures, but in subsequent periods greater use was made of their interior (Wait 1985: Chapter 5). If we were to correlate this sequence with what is known about the linear ditches, it would suggest that they had originally acted in

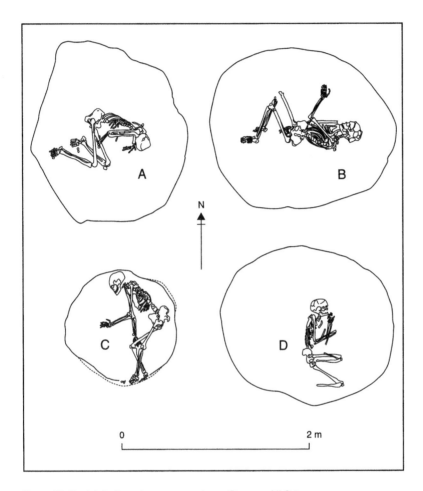

Figure 46 Burials in Iron Age storage pits at Gussage All Saints
Source: Information from Wainwright 1979b

rather the same ways as the earthworks around settlements and hill forts. Human identities may have been dispersed among the bone deposits associated with both kinds of boundary, but towards the end of this sequence the dead regained their individuality and their remains were fully integrated into the cycle of daily life. That may be why so many of them were buried in corn storage pits (Hill 1995: Chapter 11).

Taking an even longer view, it would certainly be possible to argue that special-ised deposits, including those involving human and animal remains, were increas-ingly 'domesticated'. That is to say, these kinds of material seem to have changed their associations from entirely natural features of the landscape, such as lakes and rivers, to built constructions like land boundaries and the ditches around settle-ments. After that time, deposits of a rather similar kind became a regular feature of the settlement itself, where they could even be associated with the individual houses. Thus rituals that had first developed at natural places in the countryside, some of them well away from areas of settlement, were increasingly associated with the domestic world and with the monumental architecture of the hill forts.

A comparable sequence is found in Continental Europe. Here, again, votive deposits take a largely new direction in later prehistory. It is a direction that involves a much closer equation between the ritual process and the routines of food production. In northern Europe, for example, the finds from bogs include food remains, just as they had done at the start of the local sequence. These places are also associated with finds of agricultural equipment, such as ploughs (Glob 1951). Even the famous bog bodies have been interpreted as sacrifices to the goddess of fertility (Todd 1987: 166–7). Similar arguments apply to the finds from dry land. In Sweden, Germany and the Netherlands, specialised offerings can be associated with individual houses (Capelle 1987; Therkorn 1987; Ullén 1994), whilst in Denmark the so-called 'house urns' found in Late Bronze Age cremation cemeteries do not look like the dwellings of the same period, but bear a stronger resemblance to granaries. (The ancillary buildings of the Later Bronze Age are discussed by Rasmussen and Andersen [1993].) If my interpretation of these artefacts is right, they may express the same relationship between the dead and the regeneration of the crops as the inhumations from Iron Age storage pits in Britain. There is a similar emphasis on placed deposits of agricultural equipment in the Late Bronze Age of southern Sweden, where Stålborn (1997) has com-mented on the high proportion of quern stones placed in pits. These are also a feature of the Late Bronze Age/Early Iron Age ship settings in this region. In the same area, small votive pools or springs were sometimes associated with individual settlements (Stjernquist 1997). There is less direct evidence for similar practices in Germany and France, but this is probably because the contents of excavated sites are normally treated as discarded refuse: a perspective that was commonplace in Britain until recently. Even so, it is clear that human remains are associated with settlement sites and sometimes with grain storage pits. This is especially striking, as it is clear that finds of river metalwork are less common during this period.

Taken together, these observations suggest that two important developments took place in later prehistory. First, it seems likely that for several centuries the focus of votive offerings may have changed from the sacrifice of elaborate metal-work, such as ornaments and weapons, to items that were intimately connected with the production and storage of food. At the same time, this new concern with fertility found expression in a novel setting, for many of these deposits were no longer associated exclusively with natural places on the margins of the landscape, but were located in the heart of the domestic world. The strongest evidence for these new practices comes from the hill forts of southern England, where the proportion of specialised deposits is higher than it is on other sites (Hill 1995; Wait 1985). This seems especially appropriate, as recent excavation suggests that

some of them contained shrines. Perhaps these monuments assumed the significance that had previously belonged to natural places.

That is a plausible argument, but it is one that seems oddly familiar, for it is
essentially the same as Tilley's interpretation of the creation of monuments at a
much earlier time, during the *Neolithic* period. Some of these sites are found in
virtually the same regions of Britain. The closing paragraph of *A Phenomenology of
Landscape* expresses this idea:

> What happens in the Neolithic is the constitution of a different sense of time,
> place and social identity through monument building. . . . Cultural markers
> are being used to create a new sense of place, harnessed to legitimise patterns
> of social control, restricting access to knowledge deemed essential to group
> reproduction, whilst continuing to make reference or lay claim to already
> established ancestral connections with, and pathways through, the landscape.
> *An already encultured landscape becomes refashioned, its meanings now controlled by the
> imposition of the cultural form of the constructed monument.*
>
> (Tilley 1994: 208; my emphasis)

Whilst I agree with much of this characterisation of the Neolithic, I suggest
that in fact such processes continued over a longer period and that the relationship
between monuments and natural places was much less stable. In the following
section, I shall explain why I take that view.

Two-part invention

As we have seen, the earliest votive deposits in north and north-west Europe
probably date from the Mesolithic period. The latest most likely belong to the
Early Middle Ages. These deposits are found in similar locations for the greater
part of their history, and their currency is more or less the same as that of other
significant places in the natural landscape.

It would be quite wrong to suppose that these places remained unchanged
throughout this lengthy history or that their relationship to monumental architecture took a consistent form. Rather than the orderly progression suggested so
far, this was a more volatile process, although it does seem to be true that in the
end the significance of many of these places transferred to the domestic sphere. In
order to explore these possibilities, the discussion has to consider the sequence as a
whole. Although this account focuses on the history of votive deposits, the other
uses that were made of natural places seem to have followed a similar course.

The creation of monuments, whatever their roles – sacred or secular, domestic
or ceremonial – might encapsulate some of the significance attached to natural
places, but it did not extinguish their importance. Instead, the creation of major
monuments frequently occurred in parallel with the emergence of a new generation of natural places in the landscape, as if the distinction between these two
domains was always felt to be important. That contrast provides a theme that runs

right through prehistoric Europe. Thus, in the Neolithic period, the creation of monuments at the centre of the sacred landscape ran in parallel with the deposition of specialised offerings in peripheral places such as rivers or bogs (Koch 1998). In the same way, the building of permanent memorials to the dead in the form of burial mounds may have connected certain kinds of deposit with particular people and places, but it developed at the same time as a quite different assemblage that might be found in other parts of the landscape. Thus ornaments and weapons might be associated with barrow cemeteries, whilst axe heads were deposited in water. That was especially true in the Early Bronze Age (Needham 1988). In the later Bronze Age, the provision of elaborate funerary monuments became less common and a new kind of pattern appeared. Burial mounds played a less conspicuous role, and now there was a sharper division between the artefact assemblages associated with settlements and those deposited in peripheral locations such as rivers (Bradley 1990a: Chapter 3). It is not an accident that weapons are rarely found in the occupation sites of this period. Even when they had been made there, convention seems to have dictated that they should be taken out of circulation somewhere else. In short, the inclusion of certain categories of deposit in settlements, burials or ceremonial centres seems to have required that *other kinds of material should be deposited on, or beyond, the edges of the landscape.* Thus each type of monument seems to have its counterpart in one or more types of natural place.

Those places often remained the same from one period to another, but their contents underwent much more drastic developments. Thus water finds commenced in the Mesolithic/Neolithic with a series of deposits concerned with human and animal fertility. In time, they became more closely associated with the remains of the dead and the artefacts deposited with them (Bradley 1990a: Chapters 2 and 3). In the Bronze Age, they provided the context for a still richer assemblage of artefacts, normally metalwork, but these were only occasionally associated with human bones. Finally, as the supply of exotica failed in the Early Iron Age, these sites resumed their original role as places for the small-scale sacrifice of food and agricultural tools (Bradley 1990a: Chapter 4). It was only towards the limits of this sequence that there was any real overlap between the contents of settlements or monuments and the material that was deposited in natural places. That happened first in the later Mesolithic and earlier Neolithic periods, and the same situation did not occur again until the Iron Age. Before that time, there was always an explicit contrast between what was happening in the heart of the landscape, whether at living sites or ceremonial centres, and what took place in more specialised locations around its edges.

This is not to insist on a uniform sequence throughout, for there is growing evidence of regional developments towards the end of this process. In some areas, the practice of providing offerings of weapons and other fine metalwork was renewed during the late pre-Roman Iron Age after a lengthy interval in which such items had been in short supply. These new deposits resemble those made some centuries before during the later Bronze Age, and in many cases they took place in exactly the same areas. Perhaps less formal offerings had been placed there during the intervening period. The problem is that these are less likely to have been recognised and dated.

At the limits of the Roman Empire, votive deposits became more specialised and were generally – but not always – associated with territorial boundaries and with formal temples and shrines (Roymans 1990: Chapter 4). These were in areas that eventually came under imperial rule. Outside the limits of Roman power, the sequence extended over a still longer period, and even increased in scale as the weapons of defeated war bands were committed to the waters (Hagberg 1967). Such traditions did not come to an end in northern Europe before the Early Middle Ages. Until that time, there was always a duality between the power exerted from the centres of local authority and the tradition of making offerings around the edges of the territory.

To sum up, during most of this sequence we can think in terms of contrasting archaeological assemblages. The material recovered from votive deposits was rather different from that associated with settlements and monuments. The two groups overlapped towards the opposite ends of the cycle, but, in between, the distinctions became steadily more pronounced. Monuments may have taken on some of the attributes of natural places, but these were soon replaced by other ones.

The memory of places

It is paradoxical that the same natural places should have been used over such long periods of time when political and social organisation was changing so drastically. This is especially puzzling as it is clear that the physical character of some of these locations altered too.

A good example is provided by the bog hoards of Neolithic Denmark (Koch 1998). As we saw in Chapter 4, many of these locations had lengthy histories, in some cases beginning with nearby hunting camps dating from the later Mesolithic and earlier Neolithic periods. Nearly half the locations with finds including pottery saw a continuous history of deposition extending for at least one more phase. Eight of them remained in use until the Late Neolithic, two into the Bronze Age and nine more into the Iron Age. At the same time, other places were used intermittently. This applies to just over a quarter of those originating at the beginning of the Neolithic period. In this case, there is a problem, for certain phases may be missing because of the uncertainties of recognising and recording such material. Otherwise it seems reasonable to infer that the significance of certain places was still remembered.

On a superficial level, this might suggest that the use of watery locations for votive deposits was quite a stable process, in contrast to the changing history of settlements and monuments in the wider landscape, but this is not the case. There is evidence that the earliest deposits in these locations were immersed in shallow water and that the local environment changed during this lengthy history, so that some of the later offerings were placed in peat bogs. There is rather similar evidence from another period. The great bog hoards at Skedemosse in Sweden date from the early first millennium AD, yet excavation on the same site showed that it had also been significant in the later Bronze Age when it was a major source of fish; a series of wooden traps were identified and dated in the course of fieldwork. In between, the site was used for the sacrifice of animals (Hagberg 1967, Vol. 2: Chapters 7 and 8). During this time, the environment seems to have changed and the edges of the lake became increasingly overgrown.

A very different situation arises in the case of disused monuments. I have already commented on the difficulty that people in the past may have experienced in distinguishing between natural rock formations and ruined structures. In this case, the same problem can be approached from the opposite direction. Would long-disused monuments necessarily be recognised as human constructions, or would they have acquired a significance similar to that of natural places?

A good example is provided by the metal hoards. There are a number of cases in Britain and southern Scandinavia where it is clear that these collections were directly associated with the remains of older monuments. At first sight this might have been because the importance of these places was obvious to the casual observer, but in fact that interpretation is inadequate, for more of these deposits were buried in natural mounds. There are many possible interpretations of this phenomenon. Did it happen because the barrows were considered to be of natural origin? Or did geological features become a focus for offerings because they were mistaken for burial mounds? In Denmark, there may be some patterning among these deposits (Levy 1982). Here it is the ornament hoards that are most often associated both with natural mounds and with funerary monuments. They are mainly found in Period IV when barrow burial had recently gone out of fashion, and this association lost its significance by the end of the Bronze Age. The groups of ornaments may have been the equivalent of earlier grave goods, even though these finds were not accompanied by human remains. The deposits associated with smiths can be found in the same kinds of places, but they tend to be later in date; it seems as if the changing character of the deposits reflects the passage of time since the barrows were built. The earlier hoards resemble funeral offerings, but the later deposits do not.

There is a striking parallel for this pattern in the British Isles, where Richard Hingley (1997) has observed how often the sites of abandoned monuments were used for working bronze and iron. Sometimes this happened at stone circles, which people could probably identify as human constructions. That might be why such a specialised activity took place there. But there are other sites where they could have retained a more precise memory of the original uses of these places. At Dainton in Devon, a smith seems to have been making spearheads and other weapons on the flank of an older burial mound (Needham 1980), and the same process took place on two neighbouring monuments at Loanhead of Daviot in north-east Scotland, where in both instances weapons seem to have been produced on the sites of Bronze Age cremation cemeteries (Figure 47; Kilbride Jones 1935). This may be more than a coincidence. The mould fragments from the

Figure 47 The stone circle at Loanhead of Daviot, Aberdeenshire, Scotland

long-lived monument at Loanhead of Daviot were deposited in exactly the same position as the earlier burials. A similar relationship is found at Montcrieffe and Sarn-y-bryn-Caled (Gibson 1994: 136; Stewart 1985). The mould fragments from Dainton occupied the sector of the mound where secondary cremations might be deposited during an earlier period. I have already suggested that metalworking was a specialised activity, imbued with arcane rituals. Could it be that the treatment of the raw metal was thought of as a similar process to the transformation of the body by fire?

These details are important, as they are related to human memory. How far were people aware of the distinction between barrows and natural mounds? Did their knowledge influence what they thought of as appropriate offerings? And would the smiths working at Loanhead of Daviot or Sarn-y-bryn-Caled have known of the location and character of the cremation burials on those sites? These are difficult cases, but they do identify a problem of much wider significance. Rowlands (1993) has discussed two very different ways in which memory works. One is through the commemoration of particular people, events and places by the construction of monuments. These are often intended as memorials, and they can be adapted and reused from one generation to another over long periods of time. The larger and more complex the monument, the more difficult it is to remain unaware of its past significance. It can be identified as an antiquity even if it can no longer be understood.

The other way of creating memories is through acts that leave no lasting trace behind them: acts such as the deposition of valuables or the destruction of monuments. These cannot be interpreted through any surviving remains, but the event itself is remembered and celebrated by later generations. It might be commemorated by stories and by the naming of places, and in that way the significance of particular locations could be preserved over long periods of time.

Surely it is that distinction that lies behind so much of this evidence. The locations of the Danish Neolithic hoards retained their importance, not because those places stayed the same – in fact they changed from shallow water to peat bogs – but because the individual acts of deposition were remembered and were celebrated. The same may have been true of the cremation burials on the British sites, for here identical locations were selected for another ritually charged activity involving the use of fire. More practical considerations would have played a part as well. Bronze Age barrows in Denmark could have been chosen as the sites for hoards because some of them were still identifiable as memorials to the dead, but by this time it was becoming more difficult to distinguish others from features of geological origin. These examples are unusual in posing so many problems, for often the evidence is clear-cut. The distinction between monuments and natural places may have been that between two ways of remembering the past and two ways of thinking about time.

Places and the politics of the past

I began this chapter by discussing boundaries. By now it will be clear that those boundaries are both real and metaphorical. The linear earthworks of Wessex can be followed on the ground, and their relations to settlements and hill forts can be studied by excavation. Their ditches contain a series of placed deposits just like those associated with enclosures of the same period. But the selection of these places for special attention is revealing in another way, for the finds of human and animal skulls also recall the material deposited in natural features of the land-scape. They belong at a pivotal point in a more complex sequence, and in that sense they occupy another kind of boundary.

That metaphorical division is not just between two kinds of places. In the previous section, I argued that it is also between separate ways of remembering the past. They may be subject to different degrees of social control. Chapter 7 discussed the translation of natural places into monuments, one of the key ele-ments in Tilley's interpretation. The erection of these structures may have had several effects. It directed the experience of the people who visited these places, it controlled their movements and it restricted access to certain locations. It involved the participation of a large labour force in a collective project, and it allowed some of these places to be invested with new symbolic meanings. None of this implies that the significance of these structures remained unchanged. Monuments could be adapted or rebuilt and their significance could certainly be reinterpreted, but it is surely the case that they were originally conceived with the aim of conveying ideas to a large audience: ideas that might very well extend into the future. That could not have been the case with ritual practices that left no tangible remains behind them, like the deposition of metalwork in rivers or the burial of special artefacts when their powers were extinguished. These events might have been remembered, but that had to be an active process conducted between successive generations of people if it were to have any importance. There were no visible reminders of these transactions to demand an explanation (Küchler 1987).

These two phenomena could have had quite different implications in the politics of the past. Monuments of any kind pose a challenge to the people who view them. They stand for a set of beliefs that were enshrined in a durable form by people who had certain ideas to convey and who were capable of mustering the labour forces needed to enshrine them in permanent form. At the least that process requires consensus; sometimes it depends on coercion. In either case, the finished work celebrates a shared body of knowledge that may be fundamental to local identities.

The use of more marginal locations for other kinds of transactions may have had a quite different significance. These are acts that do not depend on a large number of people (although they do not preclude them), and they are acts that leave no recognisable traces behind. They can be remembered or forgotten, misremembered or reinterpreted. In every case, their meanings can be more fluid and more difficult to control. That may be why the nature of votive deposits changes so radically at different points in its history. Such activities pose a threat to the social order, especially if they happen away from the main centres of political authority.

Perhaps that is why this duality between monuments and natural places breaks down during later prehistory. It is with the agricultural expansion of the later Bronze Age and Iron Age that we can envisage greater concentrations of population in northern and western Europe, and it is at this time that there may have been the first moves towards political centralisation, many of them precipitated by the growing influence of societies in the Mediterranean. It is when monuments seem to have been attacked and defended, when the storage of food appears to have come under some form of centralised control, and when there is clearer evidence for the emergence of elites than there had been in earlier periods. Nowhere is this more obvious than around the Roman frontier (Kristiansen 1998: Chapters 6–8).

It was at this time that the provision of votive offerings seems to have been transformed. It happened in two different ways. First, many of these practices were relocated to monuments where they could take place in a more public setting. On a local scale, this applies to the transformation of the deposits associated with fertility and food production, but it also refers to the more lavish deposits of weaponry that became such a characteristic of the Late Iron Age. This was a special feature of the temples and sanctuaries that seem to have developed at this time. The other change was the use of weapon deposits to reinforce major boundaries. That may be why there is such a clear relationship between the distribution of river finds and the borders of different polities suggested by the distribution of coins (Figure 48; Bradley 1990a: Chapter 4). The effect was to draw these rituals into a new political arena and to bring them under closer control.

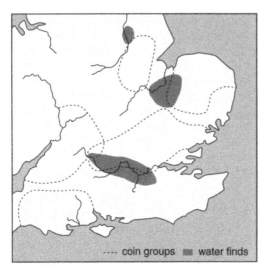

Figure 48 The distribution of Iron Age votive
deposits and territorial boundaries, as
suggested by coin distributions in England
Source: Bradley 1990a

Half a millennium later, rather similar changes took place in southern Scandinavia. The spoils taken from defeated war bands were still being deposited in the traditional locations until about 500 AD, but after this period that practice came to an end and the sacrificial bogs and lakes seem to have lost their importance (Fabech 1998). With the development of central places associated with new leaders in society, the focus of ritual activity changed and sacred sites were established in the vicinity of exceptionally rich settlements like Gudme and Uppåkra. In time, a number of these locations were occupied by Christian churches (Figure 49). As Näsman has argued, the sequence of votive deposits ended with 'the institutionalisation of the people's cult practices in the hands of the elite' (1998: 113), and votive deposits changed their distribution to the settlements where those leaders lived. That development was among the social changes that led to the formation of the state.

I have illustrated this argument with the evidence of votive deposits, but the same issues must have affected other parts of the archaeological record, as different aspects of social life came under closer control. Artefact production, for example, seems to have been increasingly located at the settlement sites and no longer happened in seclusion at special places in the landscape. By the Early Iron Age, rock art disappeared. This is not to suggest that every aspect of life had come under scrutiny, or that people had lost any capacity for individual action – it is simply a matter of degree. Natural places played a less important role in social life

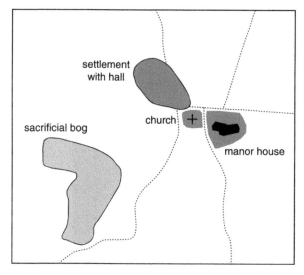

Figure 49 The siting of the votive deposit at Dejbjerg,
           Denmark, in relation to the successive high-status
           settlements on the site
Source: Information from Fabech 1998

as the activities that had occurred there moved to another setting. Their significance was not at an end entirely, but they were never to play such a prominent role again.

Perhaps it is because natural places lost some of their power in the historical period that they have lost so much of their prehistory as well. It has been the aim of this book to establish how much of it can still be recovered.

Bibliography

Alasker, S. 1987. *Bømlo – Steinalderens råstoffsentrum på Sørvestlandet*, Bergen: Bergen University Historical Museum

Alcock, S. and Osborne, R. (eds) 1994. *Placing the Gods*, Oxford: Clarendon Press

Althin, C.-A. 1945. *Studien zu den bronzezeitlichen Felszeitschungen von Skåne*, Lund: Gleerup

Anati, E. 1994. *Valcamonica Rock Art – A New History for Europe*, Capo di Ponti: Edizioni del Centro

Arafat, K. 1996. *Pausanias's Greece*, Cambridge: Cambridge University Press

Artelius, T. 1996. *Lång färd och återkomst – skeppet i bronsålders gravar*, Gothenburg: Gothenburg University Department of Archaeology

Auden, W.H. 1963. *The Dyer's Hand and Other Essays*, London: Faber and Faber

Barfield, L. and Chippindale, C. 1997. 'Meaning in the later prehistoric rock-engravings of Mont Bégo, Alpes-Maritimes, France', *Proceedings of the Prehistoric Society* 63, 103–28

Barndon, R. 1996. 'Mental and material aspects of iron working: a cultural comparative perspective', in G. Pwiti and R. Soper (eds), *Aspects of African Archaeology. Papers from the 10th Congress of the Pan-African Association for Prehistory and Related Studies*, Harare: University of Zimbabwe Publications

Barrett, J. 1994. *Fragments from Antiquity*, Oxford: Blackwell

Barrett, J., Bradley, R. and Green, M. 1991. *Landscape, Monuments and Society. The Prehistory of Cranborne Chase*, Cambridge: Cambridge University Press

Beaumont, B. (trans.) 1985. *Flaubert and Turgenev. The Complete Correspondence*, London: Athlone Press

Bender, B. (ed.) 1993. *Landscape: Politics and Perspectives*, Oxford: Berg

Berridge, P. 1993. 'Cornish axe factories: fact or fiction?', in N. Ashton and A. David (eds), *Stories in Stone*, London: Lithic Studies Society

Bertilsson, U. 1987. *The Rock Carvings of Northern Bohuslän*, Stockholm: Stockholm University Department of Archaeology

Bianco Peroni, V. 1979. 'Bronzene Gewässer- und Höhenfunde aus Italien', *Jahresbericht des Vorgeschichte der Universität Frankfurt A.M.* (1978–79), 321–35

Birge, D. 1994. 'Trees in the landscape of Pausanias' "Periegesis"', in S. Alcock and R. Osborne (eds), *Placing the Gods*, Oxford: Clarendon Press

Boardman, J. 1961. *The Cretan Collection in Oxford. The Dictaean Cave and Iron Age Crete*, Oxford: Clarendon Press

Bradley, R. 1975. 'Maumbury Rings, Dorchester: the excavations of 1908–13', *Archaeologia* 105, 1–97

Bradley, R. 1990a *The Passage of Arms. An Archaeological Analysis of Prehistoric Hoards and Votive Deposits*, Cambridge: Cambridge University Press

Bradley, R. 1990b. 'Perforated stone axeheads in the British Neolithic: their distribution and significance', *Oxford Journal of Archaeology* 9, 299–304

Bradley, R. 1993. *Altering the Earth. The Origins of Monuments in Britain and Continental Europe*, Edinburgh: Society of Antiquaries of Scotland

Bradley, R. 1997. *Rock Art and the Prehistory of Atlantic Europe*, London: Routledge

Bradley, R. 1998a. *The Significance of Monuments. On the Shaping of Human Experience in Neolithic and Bronze Age Europe*, London: Routledge

Bradley, R. 1998b. 'Daggers drawn: depictions of Bronze Age weapons in Atlantic Europe', in C. Chippindale and P. Taçon (eds), *The Archaeology of Rock Art*, Cambridge: Cambridge University Press.

Bradley, R. 1998c. 'Ruined buildings, ruined stones: enclosures, tombs and natural places in the Neolithic of south-west England', *World Archaeology* 30, 13–22

Bradley, R. 1999. 'The stony limits: rock carvings in passage graves and in the open air', in A. Harding (ed.), *Experiment and Design: Archaeological Studies in Honour of John Coles*, Oxford: Oxbow Books

Bradley, R. in press. 'The authority of abstraction: knowledge and power in the landscapes of prehistoric Europe', in K. Helsgog (ed.), *Proceedings of the Second Alta Conference on Rock Art*

Bradley, R. and Edmonds, M. 1993. *Interpreting the Axe Trade. Production and Exchange in Neolithic Britain*, Cambridge: Cambridge University Press

Bradley, R. and Fábregas, R. 1998. 'Crossing the border: contrasting styles of rock art in the prehistory of north-west Iberia', *Oxford Journal of Archaeology* 17, 287–308

Bradley, R. and Gordon, K. 1988. 'Human skulls from the River Thames, their dating and significance', *Antiquity* 62, 503–9

Bradley, R. and Thomas, J. 1984. 'Some new information on the henge monument at Maumbury Rings, Dorchester', *Proceedings of the Dorset Natural History and Archaeological Society* 106, 128–32

Bradley, R., Criado, F. and Fábregas, R. 1995. 'Rock art and the prehistoric landscape of Galicia', *Proceedings of the Prehistoric Society* 61, 142–53

Bradley, R., Entwistle, R. and Raymond, F. 1994. *Prehistoric Land Divisions on Salisbury Plain*, London: English Heritage

Bradley, R., Meredith, P., Smith, J. and Edmonds, M. 1992. 'Rock physics and the stone axe trade in Neolithic Britain', *Archaeometry* 34, 323–33

Breuil, H. 1933–35. *Les peintures rupestres schématiques de la péninsule ibérique*, four volumes, Paris: Lagny

Bridgford, S. 1997. 'Mightier than the pen? An edgewise look at Irish Bronze Age swords', in J. Carman (ed.), *Material Harm: Archaeological Studies of War and Violence*, Glasgow: Cruithne Press

Briggs, S. 1989. 'Axe-making traditions in Cumbrian stone', *Archaeological Journal* 146, 1–43

Brown, A. 1993. *Before Knossos: Arthur Evans's Travels in the Balkans and Crete*, Oxford: Ashmolean Museum

Bruen Olsen, A. and Alasker, S. 1984. 'Greenstone and diabase utilisation in the Stone Age of Western Norway', *Norwegian Archaeological Review* 17, 71–103

Budd, P. and Taylor, T. 1995. 'The faerie smith meets the bronze industry: magic versus science in the interpretation of prehistoric metal-making', *World Archaeology* 27, 133–43

Bueno Ramirez, P. and Balbín Behrmann, R. 1992. 'L'art mégalithique dans la péninsule Iberique: une vue d'ensemble', *L'Anthropologie* 96, 499–572

Bunch, B. and Fell, C. 1949. 'A stone axe factory at Pike o' Stickle, Great Langdale, Westmorland', *Proceedings of the Prehistoric Society* 15, 1–20

Burenhult, G. 1980. *Götalands hällristningar*, Stockholm: Stockholm University Institute of Archaeology

Burkert, W. 1985. *Greek Religion: Archaic and Classical*, Oxford: Blackwell

Burton, J. 1984. 'Quarrying in a tribal society', *World Archaeology* 16, 234–47

Buxton, R. 1994. *Imaginary Greece. The Contexts of Mythology*, Cambridge: Cambridge University Press

Capelle, T. 1987. 'Eisenzeitliche Bauopfer', *Frühmittelalterliche Studien* 21, 182–205

Capelle, T. 1995. 'Bronze Age stone ships', in O. Crumlin-Pedersen and B. Thye (eds), *The Ship as Symbol*, Copenhagen: National Museum of Denmark

Carmichael, D., Hubert, J., Reeves, B. and Schanche, A. (eds) 1994. *Sacred Sites, Sacred Places*, London: Routledge

Case, H. 1993. 'Beakers: deconstruction and after', *Proceedings of the Prehistoric Society* 59, 241–68

Chappell, S. 1987. *Stone Axe Morphology and Distribution in Northern Britain*, Oxford: British Archaeological Reports (BAR British Series 177)

Charlton, B. and Mitchelson, M. 1983. 'Yardhope. A shrine to Cocidius?', *Britannia* 14, 143–53

Childe, V.G. 1958. *The Prehistory of European Society*, Harmondsworth: Penguin

Claris, P. and Quartermaine, J. 1989. 'The Neolithic quarries and axe factory sites of Great Langdale and Scafell Pike: a new field survey', *Proceedings of the Prehistoric Society* 55, 1–25

Cleal, R. 1988. 'The occurrence of drilled holes in later Neolithic pottery', *Oxford Journal of Archaeology* 7, 139–45

Cleal, R. 1995. 'Pottery fabrics in Wessex in the fourth to second millennia BC', in I. Kinnes and G. Varndell (eds), *'Unbaked Urns of Rudely Shape': Essays on British and Irish Pottery for Ian Longworth*, Oxford: Oxbow

Cleal, R., Walker, K. and Montague, R. 1995. *Stonehenge in its Landscape. Twentieth-Century Exacavations*, London: English Heritage

Clottes, J. 1996. 'Recent studies in Palaeolithic art', *Cambridge Archaeological Journal* 6, 179–89

Coles, J. 1999. 'The dancer on the rock: record and analysis at Järrestad, Sweden', *Proceedings of the Prehistoric Society* 65

Collado, G.H., Fernández Algaba, M., Pozuelo Lorenzo, D. and Grión Abumalham, M. 1997. 'Pinturas rupestres esquemáticas en la transición del IV al III milenio a. C.: el abrigo de la Charneca Chica (Oliva de Mérida, Badajoz)', *Trabajos de Prehistoria* 54.2, 143–9

Commendador Rey, B. 1995. 'Caracterización de la metalurgia inical gallego: una revisión', *Trabajos de Prehistoria* 52.2, 111–29

Cooney, G. 1998. 'Breaking stones, making places: the social landscape of the axe production site', in A. Gibson and D. Simpson (eds), *Prehistoric Ritual and Religion*, Stroud: Sutton

Cooney, G. and Mandal, S. 1998. *The Irish Stone Axe Project, Monograph 1*, Dublin: Wordwell.

Corlett, C. 1997. 'Prehistoric pilgramage to Croagh Patrick', *Archaeology Ireland* 11.2, 8–11

Costas Goberna, F.J. and Pereira García, E. 1998. 'Los grabados rupestres en épocas históricas', in F.J. Costas Goberna and J.M. Hidalgo Cuñarro (eds), *Reflexiones sobre el arte prehistórico de Galicia*, Vigo: Associación Arqueológica Viguesa

Crumlin-Pedersen, O. and Thye, B. (eds) 1995. *The Ship as Symbol*, Copenhagen: National Museum of Denmark.

Cunliffe, B. 1991. *Iron Age Communities in Britain*, Third edition. London: Routledge

Damm, C. 1998. 'Rituals: symbols and action?' in A.-C. Andersson, A. Gilberg, O. Jensen, J. Karlsson and M. Rolöf (eds), *The Kaleidoscopic Past*, Gothenburg: Gothenburg University Department of Archaeology

David, A. and Williams, G. 1995. 'Stone axe-head manufacture: new evidence from the Preseli Hills, Wales', *Proceedings of the Prehistoric Society* 61, 433–60

De Grooth, M. 1997. 'Social and economic interpretations of the chert procurement strategies of the Bandkeramik settlement at Hienheim, Bavaria', *Analecta Praehistorica Leidensia* 29, 91–8

De Lumley, H. 1995. *Le grandiose et le sacré. Gravures protohistoriques et historiques de la région du Mont Bego*, Paris: Epona

Derks, T. 1998. *Gods, Temples and Ritual Practices: the Transformation of Religious Ideas in Roman Gaul*, Amsterdam: Amsterdam University Press

Dotzler, G. 1984. *Ornament als Zeichen. Methodologische Probleme der archäologischen Interpretation*, Frankfurt: Peter Lang

Durden, T. 1995. 'The production of specialised flintwork in the later Neolithic: a case study from the Yorkshire Wolds', *Proceedings of the Prehistoric Society* 61, 409–32

Edlund, I. 1987. *The Gods and the Place: Location and Function of Sanctuaries in the Countryside of Etruria and Magna Grecia 700–400 BC*, Stockholm: Aström

Edmonds, M. 1995. *Stone Tools and Society*, London: Batsford

Edwards, G. and Bradley, R. 1999. 'Rock carvings and Neolithic artefacts on Ilkley Moor, West Yorkshire', in R. Cleal and A. MacSween (eds), *Grooved Ware in Context*, Oxford: Oxbow Books

Eliade, M. 1954. *The Myth of the Eternal Return*, London: Arkana

Eliade, M. 1964. *Shamanism*, London: Arkana

Ellen, R. 1996. 'Introduction', in R. Ellen and K. Fukui (eds), *Redefining Nature*, Oxford: Berg

Ellis, H. 1943. *The Road to Hel. A Study of the Conception of the Dead in Old Norse Literature*, Cambridge: Cambridge University Press

Elsner, J. 1995. *Art and the Roman Viewer*, Cambridge: Cambridge University Press

Eogan, G. 1983. *The Hoards of the Irish Later Bronze Age*, Dublin: University College, Dublin

Esparza Arroyo, A. 1977. 'El castro zamorano de El Pedroso y sus insculturas', *Boletín del Seminario de Estudios de Arte y Arqueología Valladolid*, 27–39

Evans, A. 1901. *The Mycenean Tree and Pillar Cult and its Mediterranean Relations; with Illustrations from Recent Cretan Finds*, London: Macmillan

Evans, C. 1994. 'Natural wonders and national monuments: a meditation upon the fate of the Tolmen', *Antiquity* 66, 200–8

Evans, J. 1943. *Time and Chance. The Story of Arthur Evans and his Forbears*, London: Longman, Green

Fabech, C. 1998. 'Kult og Samfund i yngre jernalder – Ravlunda som eksempel', in L. Larsson and B. Hårdh (eds), *Centrale platser, centrala Frågor. Samhällsstrukturen under järnaldern*, Lund: Almquist and Wiksell

Fredsjö, A. 1971. *Hällrinsningar Kville härad i Bohuslän. Svenneby socken*, Gothenburg: Gothenburg University Institute of Archaeology

Fredsjö, A. 1975 *Hällrinsningar härad i Bohuslän. Bottna socken*, Gothenburg: Gothenburg University Institute of Archaeology

Fredsjö, A. 1981. *Hällrinsningar härad i Bohuslän*, Gothenburg: Gothenburg University Institute of Archaeology

Gamble, C. 1991. 'The social context of European palaeolithic art', *Proceedings of the Prehistoric Society* 57.1, 3–15

García Alén, A. and Peña Santos, A. 1980. *Grabados rupestres de la provincia de Pontevedra*, Pontevedra: Museo de Pontevedra

García Arranz, J. 1990. *La pintura rupestre esquemática en le comerca de Las Villuercas, Cáceres*, Salamanca: Diputación de Salamanca

Gardiner, J. 1990. 'Flint procurement and Neolithic axe production on the South Downs: a reassessment', *Oxford Journal of Archaeology* 9, 119–40

Garnett, R. (ed) 1862. *Relics of Shelley*, London: Edward Moxon

Gibbs, L. 1987. 'Identifying gender representation in the archaeological record: a contextual study', in I. Hodder (ed.), *The Archaeology of Contextual Meanings*, Cambridge: Cambridge University Press

Gibson, A. 1994. 'Excavations at the Sarn-y-bryn-Caled cursus complex, Welshpool, Powys, and the timber circles of Great Britain and Ireland', *Proceedings of the Prehistoric Society* 60, 143–223

Glob, P. 1951. *Ard og plov i Nordens oldtid*, Aarhus: Jutland Archaeological Society

Green, C. 1997. 'The provenance of rocks used in the construction of Stonehenge', in B. Cunliffe and C. Renfrew (eds), *Science and Stonehenge*, London: British Academy

Green, M. and Allen, M. 1997. 'An early prehistoric shaft in Cranborne Chase', *Oxford Journal of Archaeology* 16, 121–32

Gregory, C. 1980. 'Gifts to men and gifts to gods: gift exchange and capital accumulation in contemporary Papua', *Man* 25, 628–52

Grogan, E., Condit, T., O'Carroll, F., O'Sullivan, A. and Daly, A. 1996. 'Tracing the late prehistoric landscape in North Munster', *Discovery Programme Reports* 4, 26–46. Dublin: Royal Irish Academy

Habicht, C. 1985. *Pausanias's Guide to Greece*, Berkeley: University of California Press

Hagberg, U.-E. 1967. *The Archaeology of Skedemosse.*, Two volumes, Stockholm: Almquist and Wiksell

Hänsel, A. and Hänsel, B. 1997. *Gaben an die Götter*, Berlin: Staatliche Museum zu Berlin

Hansen, S. 1991. *Studien zu den Metalldeponierungen während der Urnenfelderzeit im Rhein-Main-gebiet*, Bonn: Habelt

Harrison, R., Jackson, R. and Naphan, M., 1999. 'A rich Bell Beaker burial from Wellington Quarry, Marden, Bedfordshire', *Oxford Journal of Archaeology* 18, 1–16

Hayes, R. 1987. 'Archaeological finds in the Ryedale Windypits', *Studies in Spelaeology* 7, 31–74

Healy, F. and Housley, R. 1992. 'Nancy was not alone: skeletons of the Early Bronze Age from the Norfolk peat fens', *Antiquity* 66, 948–55

Helsgog, K. 1987. 'Selective depictions. A study of 3,500 years of rock carvings from Arctic Norway and their relationship to the Saami drums', in I. Hodder (ed.), *Archaeology as Long-term History*, Cambridge: Cambridge University Press

Helsgog, K. 1988. *Helleristningene i Alta*, Alta: Alta Museum

Helsgog, K. 1997. 'La conexión costera. Le percepción del paisaje y los grabados rupestres en el norte de Europa', in F.J. Costas Goberna and J.M. Hidalgo Cuñarro (eds), *Los motivos de fauna y armas en los grabados prehistóricos del continente Europeo*, Vigo: Asocación Arqueológica Viguesa

Herbert, E. 1984. *Red Gold of Africa*, Madison: University of Wisconsin Press

Herity, M. 1974. *Irish Passage Graves*, Dublin: Irish Universities Press

Hill, J.D. 1995. *Ritual and Rubbish in the Iron Age of Wessex*, Oxford: British Archaeological Reports (BAR British Series 242)

Hingley, R. 1997. 'Ironworking and regeneration. A study of the symbolic meaning of metalworking in Iron Age Britain', in A. Gwilt and C. Haselgrove (eds), *Reconstructing Iron Age Societies*, Oxford: Oxbow

Hirsch, E. and O' Hanlon, M. (eds) 1995. *The Anthropology of Landscape*, Oxford: Clarendon Press

Hodder, I. 1982a. *Symbols in Action*, Cambridge: Cambridge University Press.

Hodder 1982b. 'Sequences of structural change in the Dutch Neolithic', in I. Hodder (ed.), *Symbolic and Structural Archaeology*, Cambridge: Cambridge University Press

Hogarth, D.G. 1900. 'The Dictaean Cave', *Annual of the British School at Athens* 6, 94–116

Hood, B. 1988. 'Sacred pictures, sacred rocks: ideological and social space in the North Norwegian Stone Age', *Norwegian Archaeological Review* 21, 65–84

Hulthén, B. 1984. 'The Carrowmore pottery: a technological study', in G. Burenhult (ed.), *The Archaeology of Carrowmore*, Stockholm: Stockholm University Institute of Archaeology

Ingold, T. 1986. *The Appropriation of Nature*, Manchester: Manchester University Press

Innselset, S. 1995. 'Skålgropristningar. Ein analyse av hellerristningane i Valdres', MA thesis University of Bergen

Itkonen, T. 1944. *Heidenische Religion und späterer Aberlauge bei den Finnischen Lappen*, Helsinki: Suomalais Ugrilainen

Johansen, Ø. 1979. 'Results of a new investigation of the Bronze Age rock carvings', *Norwegian Archaeological Review* 12, 108–14

Jones, A. 1998. 'Where eagles dare: landscape, animals and the Neolithic of Orkney', *Journal of Material Culture* 3, 301–24

Jorge, V.O. 1998. 'Interpreting the "megalithic art" of western Iberia: some preliminary remarks', *Journal of Iberian Archaeology*, 69–83

Jost, M. 1994. 'The distribution of sanctuaries in civic space in Arkadia', in S. Alcock and R. Osborne (eds), *Placing the Gods*, Oxford: Clarendon Press

Karelsou, A. 1981. 'The peak sanctuary at Mount Juktas', in R. Hägg and N. Marinatos (eds), *Sanctuaries and Cults in the Aegean Bronze Age*, Stockholm: P. Astrōm Förlag

Kaul, F. 1995. 'Ships on bronzes', in O. Crumlin-Pedersen and B. Thye (eds), *The Ship as Symbol*, Copenhagen: National Museum of Denmark

Kaul, F. 1997. 'Skibet og solhesten. Om nye fund af bronzealderens religiøse kunst', *Nationalmuseets Arbejdsmark*, 101–14

Kilbride Jones, H. 1935. 'An account of the stone circle at Loanhead of Daviot', *Proceedings of the Society of Antiquaries of Scotland* 69, 168–222

Kinnes, I., Gibson, A., Ambers, J., Bowman, S. and Boast, R. 1991. 'Radiocarbon dating and British Beakers', *Scottish Archaeological Review* 8, 35–68

Koch, E. 1998. *Neolithic Bog Pots from Zealand, Møn, Lolland and Falster*, Copenhagen: Nordiske Fortidsminder Serie B

Koch, E. 1999. 'Neolithic offerings from the wetlands of eastern Denmark', in B. Coles, J. Coles and M. Schou Jørgensen (eds), *Bog Bodies, Sacred Sites and Wetland Archaeology*, Exeter: Wetland Archaeological Research Project

Kopytoff, I. 1986. 'The cultural biography of things: commoditisation as process', in A. Appadurai (ed.), *The Social Life of Things*, Cambridge: Cambridge University Press.

Kristiansen, K. 1978. 'The consumption of wealth in Bronze Age Denmark', in K. Kristiansen and C. Paludan-Müller (eds), *New Directions in Scandinavian Archaeology*, Copenhagen: National Museum of Denmark

Kristiansen, K. 1987. 'Centre and periphery in Bronze Age Scandinavia', in M. Rowlands, M. Larsen and K. Kristiansen (eds), *Centre and Periphery in the Ancient World*, Cambridge: Cambridge University Press

Kristiansen, K. 1998. *Europe before History*, Cambridge: Cambridge University Press

Kubach, W. 1983. 'Bronzezeitliche Deponierungen in Nordhessischen sowie im Weser-und Leinerbergland', *Jahrbuch des Römisch-Germanischen Zentralmuseums Mainz*, 113–59

Küchler, S. 1987. 'Malangan: art and memory in a Melanesian society', *Man* 22, 238–55

Lanting, J. and Van der Waals, J.D. 1981. 'Some comments on radiocarbon dating and British Beakers', *Scottish Archaeological Review* 8, 69–70

Larsson, T. 1986. *The Bronze Age Metalwork in Southern Sweden. Aspects of Social and Spatial Organization 1800–500 BC*, Umeå: Umeå University Department of Archaeology

Lawson, E.T. and McCauley, R. 1990. *Rethinking Religion. Connecting Cognition and Culture*, Cambridge: Cambridge University Press

Levi, P. 1971. 'Introduction', in P. Levi (trans.), *Pausanias, Guide to Greece*, vol. 1, 1–5, London: Penguin

Levy, J. 1982. *Social and Religious Organisation in Bronze Age Denmark. An Analysis of Ritual Hoard Finds*, Oxford: British Archaeological Reports (BAR International Series 124)

Lewis, I. 1986. *Religion in Context. Cults and Charisma*, Cambridge: Cambridge University Press

Lewis, I. 1989. *Ecstatic Religion. A Study of Shamanism and Spirit Possession*, Second edition, London: Routledge

Lewis Williams, D. and Dowson, T. 1988. 'The signs of all times: entoptic phenomena in Upper Palaeolithic art', *Current Anthropology* 29, 201–45

Linders, T. and Nordquist, G. (eds) 1987. *Gifts to the Gods*, Uppsala: Uppsala Studies in Ancient Mediterranean and Near Eastern Civilization

Lock, G. and Stancic, Z. (eds) 1995. *Archaeology and Geographical Information Systems*, London: Taylor and Francis

Lødøn, T. 1998. 'Interpreting Mesolithic axe deposits from a region of western Norway', *Archaeologia Baltica* 3, 195–204

Maier, R. 1977. 'Urgeschichtliche Opferreste einer Felsplate und einer Schachthöhle der Fränkischen Alb', *Germania* 55, 295–313

Malmer, M. 1981. *A Chorological Study of North European Rock Art*, Stockholm: Almquist and Wiksell

Mandt, G. 1995. 'Alternative analogies in rock art interpretation: the West Norwegian case', in K. Helsgog and B. Olsen (eds), *Perceiving Rock Art: Social and Political Perspectives*, Oslo: Novus forlag

Manker, E. 1957. *Lapparnas heliga ställen*, Stockholm: Nordiska Museet

Martin Valls, R. 1983. 'Las insculturas del castro de Yecla da Yelta y sus relaciones con los petroglifos gallegos', *Zephyrus* 36, 217–31

Martinez García, J. 1995. 'Grabados prehistoricos, grabados historicos. Reflexiones sobre un debate a superar', *Revista de Arqueologia* 172, 14–23

Meillassoux, C. 1968. 'Ostentation, destruction, reproduction', *Economie et Société* 1, 93–105

Mercer, R. 1981. 'Excavations at Carn Brea, Illogan, Cornwall', *Cornish Archaeology* 20, 1–204

Mitchell, F. 1992. 'Notes on some non-local cobbles at the entrances to the passage graves at Newgrange and Knowth, County Meath', *Journal of the Royal Society of Antiquaries of Ireland* 122, 128–45

Moore, J. 1996. *Architecture and Power in the Ancient Andes: the Archaeology of Public Buildings*, Cambridge: Cambridge University Press

Mordant, C., Pernot, M. and Rychner, V. (eds) 1998. *L'atelier de bronzier en Europe*, Paris: CTHS

Morgan, L. 1988. *The Miniature Wall Paintings of Thera. A Study in Aegean Culture and Iconography*, Cambridge: Cambridge University Press

Morphy, H. 1991. *Ancestral Connections*, Chicago: Chicago University Press

Mulk, I.-M. 1994. 'Sacrificial places and their meaning in Saami society', in D. Carmichael, J. Hubert, B. Reeves and A. Schanche (eds), *Sacred Sites, Sacred Places*, London: Routledge

Mulk, I.-M. 1996. 'The role of the Sámi in fur trading during the Late Iron Age and Nordic medieval period in the light of Sámi sacrificial sites in Lapland', *Acta Borealia* 13, 47–80

Murdoch, J. 1984. *The Discovery of the Lake District*, London: Victoria and Albert Museum

Nash, G. (ed) 1997. *Semiotics of Landscape: Archaeology of Mind*, Oxford: British Archaeological Reports (BAR International Series 661)

Näsman, U. 1998. 'The Scandinavians' view of Europe in the Migration Period', in L. Larsson and B. Stjernquist (eds), *The World-View of Prehistoric Man*, Lund: Almquist and Wiksell

Needham, S. 1980. 'An assemblage of Late Bronze Age metalworking debris from Dainton, Devon', *Proceedings of the Prehistoric Society* 46, 177–215

Needham, S. 1988. 'Selective deposition in the British Early Bronze Age', *World Archaeology* 20, 229–48

Needham, S. and Burgess, C. 1980. 'The Later Bronze Age in the lower Thames valley: the metalwork evidence', in J. Barrett and R. Bradley (eds), *Settlement and Society in the British Later Bronze Age*, Oxford: British Archaeological Reports (BAR British Series 83)

Nordbladh, J. 1980. *Glyfer och rum. Kring hällristningar i Kville*, Gothenburg: Gothenburg University Department of Archaeology

Nowicki, K. 1994. 'Some remarks on Pre- and Protopalatial peak sanctuaries in Crete', *Aegean Archaeology* 1, 31–48

O'Kelly, M.J. 1982. *Newgrange. Archaeology, Art and Legend*, London: Thames and Hudson

Pausanias (trans. J. Frazer) 1898. *Description of Greece*, London: Macmillan

Peatfield, A. 1992. 'Rural ritual in Bronze Age Crete: the peak sanctuary at Atsiphades', *Cambridge Archaeological Journal* 2, 59–87

Peatfield, A. 1996. 'After the "big bang" – what? Or Minoan symbols and shrines beyond palatial collapse', in S. Alcock and R. Osborne (eds), *Placing the Gods*, Oxford: Clarendon Press

Piggott, S. 1962. *The West Kennet Long Barrow: Excavations 1955–56*, London: HMSO

Pollard, J. 1992. 'The Sanctuary, Overton Hill, Wiltshire: a re-examination', *Proceedings of the Prehistoric Society* 58, 213–26

Pollard, J. 1995. 'Structured deposition at Woodhenge', *Proceedings of the Prehistoric Society* 61, 137–56

Poulsen, F. 1920. *Delphi*, London: Gyldendal

Pryor, F. (ed) 1992. 'Current research at Flag Fen', *Antiquity* 66, 439–531

Randsborg, K. 1993. 'Kivik. Archaeology and iconography', *Acta Archaeologica* 64.1, 1–147

Rasmussen, M. and Andersen, C. 1993. 'Bronze Age settlement', in B. Storgaard (ed.), *Digging into the Past – 25 Years of Danish Archaeology*, Aarhus: Jutland Archaeology Society

Reid, A. and MacLean, R. 1995. 'Symbolism and social context of iron production in Karagwe', *World Archaeology* 27, 144–61

Renfrew, C. 1973. 'Monuments, mobilisation and social organisation in Neolithic Wessex', in C. Renfrew (ed.), *The Explanation of Culture Change*, London: Duckworth

Renfrew, C. 1986. 'Varna and the emergence of wealth in prehistoric Europe', in A. Appadurai (ed.), *The Social Life of Things*, Cambridge: Cambridge University Press

Richards, C. 1996a. 'Henges and water: towards an elemental understanding of monumentality and landscape in the Late Neolithic Britain', *Journal of Material Culture* 1, 313–36

Richards, C. 1996b. 'Monuments as landscape: creating the centre of the world in Late Neolithic Orkney', *World Archaeology* 28, 190–208

Richards, C. and Thomas, J. 1984. 'Ritual activity and structured deposition in Late Neolithic Wessex', in R. Bradley and J. Gardiner (eds), *Neolithic Studies*, Oxford: British Archaeological Reports (BAR British Series 133)

Rowlands, M. 1993. 'The role of memory in the transmission of culture', *World Archaeology* 25, 141–51

Roymans, N. 1990. *Tribal Societies in Northern Gaul*, Amsterdam: Cingula 12

Rudebeck, E. 1998. 'Flint extraction, axe offering and the value of cortex', in M. Edmonds and C. Richards (eds), *Understanding the Neolithic of North-western Europe*, Glasgow: Cruithne Press

Rutkowski, B. 1986. *The Cult Places of the Aegean*, New Haven: Yale University Press

Rutkowski, B. and Nowicki, K. 1996. *The Psychro Cave and Other Sacred Grottoes in Crete*, Warsaw: Polish Academy of Sciences

Rydving, H. 1995. *The End of Drum-time*, Second edition, Uppsala: Acta Universitatis Upsaliensis

Sanches, M.J. 1997. *Pré-história recente de Trás-os-Montes e alto Douro*, Porto: Sociedade Portuguesa de Antropologia e Etnologia

Sanches, M.J., Santos, P.M., Bradley, R. and Fábregas, R. 1998. 'Land marks – a new approach to the rock art of Trás-os-Montes, northern Portugal', *Journal of Iberian Archaeology* (1998), 85–104

Santos Estévez, M. 1998. 'Los espacios del arte: el diseño del panel y la articulación del paisaje en el arte rupestre gallego', *Trabajos de Prehistoria* 55.2, 73–88

Santos Estévez, M., Parcero Oubliña, C. and Criado Boado, F. 1997. 'De la arqueología symbólica del paisaje a la arqueología des los paisajes sagrados', *Trabajos de Prehistoria* 54.2, 61–80

Saville, A. 1990. *Hazleton North*, London: English Heritage

Schauer, P. 1981. 'Urnenfelderzeitliche Opferplatze in Höhlen und Felsspalten', in H. Lorenz (ed.), *Studien zur Bronzezeit*, Mainz: Von Zabern

Schefferus, J. 1956 (1673). *Lapponia*, Stockholm. Reprinted as *Acta Lapponica* 8

Schwegler, U. 1997. 'Felseichungen von Carshenna, Gemeinde Sils im Domsleschg', *Helvetica Archaeologica* 11/112, 76–126

Scourse, J. 1997. 'Transport of the Stonehenge bluestones: testing the glacial hypothesis', in B. Cunliffe and C. Renfrew (eds), *Science and Stonehenge*, London: British Academy

Scully, V. 1962. *The Earth, the Temple and the Gods: Greek Sacred Architecture*, New Haven: Yale University Press

Shee Twohig, E. 1988. 'The rock carvings at Roughting Linn, Northumberland', *Archaeologia Aeliana* 16, 37–46

Simon Marco, F. 1992. 'La religiosidad en la Céltica hispana', in M. Almagro Gorbea (ed.), *Las Céltas: Hispania y Europa*, Madrid: Universidad Complutense

Skaarup, J. 1995. 'Stone Age burials in boats', in O. Crumlin-Pedersen and B. Thye (eds), *The Ship as Symbol*, Copenhagen: National Museum of Denmark

Smith, I. 1965. *Windmill Hill and Avebury*, Oxford: Clarendon Press

Smith, I. and Simpson, D. 1964. 'Excavation of three Roman tombs and a prehistoric pit on Overton Down', *Wiltshire Archaeological Magazine* 69, 68–85

Smith, I. and Simpson, D. 1966. 'Excavation of a round barrow on Overton Hill, north Wiltshire, England', *Proceedings of the Prehistoric Society* 32, 122–55

Sognnes, K. 1998. 'Symbols in a changing world: rock art and the transition from hunting to farming in mid Norway', in C. Chippindale and P. Taçon (eds), *The Archaeology of Rock Art*, Cambridge: Cambridge University Press

Stålborn, U. 1997. 'Waste or what? Rubbish pits or ceremonial deposits at the Pryssgården site in the Late Bronze Age', *Lund Archaeological Review* 3, 21–36

Stanton, W. 1986. 'Natural sinkholes affecting the Priddy Circles', *Proceedings of the University of Bristol Spelaeological Society* 17, 355–8

Stevenson, J. 1997. 'The prehistoric rock carvings of Argyll', in G. Ritchie (ed.), *The Archaeology of Argyll*, Edinburgh: Edinburgh University Press

Stewart, M. 1985. 'The excavation of a henge, stone circle and metal working area at Montcrieffe, Perthshire', *Proceedings of the Society of Antiquaries of Scotland* 115, 125–50

Stjernquist, B. 1997. *The Röekillorna Spring. Spring-cults in Scandinavian Prehistory*, Lund: Almquist and Wiksell

Storli, I. 1996. 'On the historiography of Saami reindeer pastoralism', *Acta Borealia* 13, 81–115

Strang, V. 1997. *Uncommon Ground. Cultural Landscapes and Environmental Values*, Oxford: Berg

Strömberg, M. 1961. 'Die bronzezeitlichen Schiffssetzungen im Norden', *Meddelanden från Lunds Universitets Histroiska Museum*, 82–106

Taylor, R. 1993. *Hoards of the Bronze Age in Southern Britain: Analysis and Interpretation*, Oxford: British Archaeological Reports (BAR British Series 228)

Terebikhin, N. 1993. 'Cultural geography and the cosmography of the Saami', *Acta Borealia* 10, 3–17

Therkorn, L. 1987. 'The inter-relationship of materials and meanings: some suggestions on housing concerns in the Iron Age of Noord-Holland', in I. Hodder (ed.), *The Archaeology of Contextual Meanings*, Cambridge: Cambridge University Press

Thomas, E. 1920. *Collected Poems*, London: Selwyn and Blount

Thomas, J. 1990. 'Monuments from the inside: the case of Irish megalithic tombs', *World Archaeology* 22, 168–78

Thomas, J. 1991. *Rethinking the Neolithic*, Cambridge: Cambridge University Press

Thomas, J. 1996. *Time, Culture and Identity*, London: Routledge

Thomas, K. 1983. *Man and the Natural World. Changing Attitudes in England 1500–1800*, London: Allen Lane

Thorpe, R., Williams-Thorpe, O., Jenkins, D. and Watson, J. 1991. 'The geological sources and transport of the bluestones at Stonehenge', *Proceedings of the Prehistoric Society* 57.2, 103–57

Tilley, C. 1991a. *Material Culture and Text. The Art of Ambiguity*, London: Routledge

Tilley, C. 1991b. 'Constructing a ritual landscape', in K. Jennbert, L. Larsson, R. Petré and B. Wyszomiska-Werbart (eds), *Regions and Reflections. In Honour of Märta Strömberg*, Lund: Almquist and Wiksell

Tilley, C. 1994. *A Phenomenology of Landscape*, Oxford: Berg

Tilley, C. 1996. 'The power of rocks: topography and monument construction on Bodmin Moor', *World Archaeology* 28, 161–76

Todd, M. 1987. *The Northern Barbarians 100 BC–AD 300*, Oxford: Blackwell

Torrence, R. 1986. *Production and Exchange of Stone Tools*, Cambridge: Cambridge University Press

Traherne, T. 1903. *The Poetical Works of Thomas Traherne*, London: Dobell

Treherne, P. 1995. 'The warrior's beauty: the masculine body and self-identity in Bronze Age Europe', *Journal of European Archaeology* 3.1, 103–44

Tyree, E. 1974. *Cretan Sacred Caves*, Ann Arbor: University Microfilms

Ucko, P. and Layton, R. (eds) 1999. *The Archaeology and Anthropology of Landscape*, London: Routledge

Ullén, I. 1994. 'The power of case studies. Interpretation of a Late Bronze Age settlement in central Sweden', *Journal of European Archaeology* 2.2, 249–62

Van Hoek, M. 1997. 'Petroglyphs of south-east Monaghan, Ireland', *Adoranten*, 39–45

Villoch Vazquez, V. 1995. 'Monumentos y petroglifos: la construcción del espacio en la sociedades constructoras de tumulos del Noroeste penninsular', *Trabajos de Prehistoria* 52.1, 39–55

Vitebsky, P. 1995. *The Shaman*, London: Macmillan

Vorren, Ø. and Eriksen, H.K. 1993. *Samiske offerplaser i Varanger*, Tromsø: Nordkalott-Forlaget

Wainwright, G. 1973. 'The excavation of prehistoric and Romano-British settlements at Eaton Heath, Norwich', *Archaeological Journal* 130, 1–43

Wainwright, G. 1975. 'Religion and settlement in Wessex 3000–1700 BC', in P. Fowler (ed.), *Recent Work in Rural Archaeology*, Bradford-on-Avon: Moonraker Press

Wainwright, G. 1979a. *Mount Pleasant, Dorset: Excavations 1970–71*, London: Society of Antiquaries

Wainwright, G. 1979b. *Gussage All Saints: An Iron Age Settlement in Dorset*, London: HMSO

Wainwright, G. 1989. *The Henge Monuments*, London: Thames and Hudson

Wainwright, G. and Longworth, I. 1971. *Durrington Walls Excavations 1966–1968*, London: Society of Antiquaries

Wait, G. 1985. *Ritual and Religion in the Iron Age*, Oxford: British Archaeological Reports (BAR British Series 149)

Watrous, L.V. 1996. *The Cave Sanctuary of Zeus at Psychro*, Liège: Université de Liège, Histoire de l'art et archéologie de la Grèce antique

Watson, A. 1995. 'Investigating the distribution of Group VI debitage in the central Lake District', *Proceedings of the Prehistoric Society* 61, 661–2

Wels-Weyrauch, U. 1978. *Die Anhänge und Halsringe in Südwestdeutschland und Nordbayern*, Munich: C.H. Beck

Wels-Weyrauch, U. 1991. *Die Anhänge in Südbayern*, Stuttgart: Franz Steiner Verlag

Whitley, D. 1998. 'Finding rain in the desert: landscape, gender and far western North American rock art', in C. Chippindale and P. Taçon (eds), *The Archaeology of Rock Art*, Cambridge: Cambridge University Press

Whittle, A. 1990. 'A pre-enclosure burial at Windmill Hill, Wiltshire', *Oxford Journal of Archaeology* 9, 25–8

Whittle, A. 1997. *Sacred Mound, Holy Rings: Silbury Hill and the West Kennet Palisade Enclosures*, Oxford: Oxbow

Whittle, A. and Pollard, J. 1998. 'Windmill Hill causewayed enclosure: the harmony of symbols', in M. Edmonds and C. Richards (eds), *Understanding the Neolithic of North-Western Europe*, Glasgow: Cruithne Press

Williams, B. 1990. 'The archaeology of Rathlin Island', *Archaeology Ireland* 4, 47–51

Yates, T. 1987. 'Habitus and social space: some suggestions about meaning in the Saami (Lapp) tent *c.* 1700–1900', in I. Hodder (ed.), *The Meanings of Things*, London: Unwin Hyman

Yates, T. 1993. 'Frameworks for an archaeology of the body', in C. Tilley (ed.), *Interpretative Archaeology*, Oxford: Blackwell

Zachrisson, I. 1984. *De Samiska metalldepåerna år 1000–1350*, Umeå: Umeå University Department of Archaeology

Zipf, G. 1949. *Human Behaviour and the Principle of Least Effort*, New York: Addison Wesley

Zvelebil, M. 1997. 'Hunter-gatherer ritual landscapes: social structure and ideology among hunter-gatherers of northern Europe and western Siberia', *Analecta Praehistorica Leidensia* 29, 33–50

Index